Faith, Family, and Fortitude

The Journey of a Lifetime

Richard & Natalie Jaworski

Dear Melissa

We hope our stories

are a blessing to you

Love

Aunt Natalie + Uncle Richard

Faith, Family, and Fortitude

The Journey of a Lifetime

© 2024 by Richard and Natalie Jaworski.

Join us at DiscoverFaith.com

Scriptures Isaiah 44:21-22, John 21, Isaiah 44:3-5, Hebrews 12:22-23, Haggai 2:18-19: St. Joseph Edition of The New American Bible © 1970. 1 Corinthians 10:13: New American Bible Revised Edition. Isaiah 65:21, Psalm 23:4: English Standard Version. Philippians 4:13: New King James Version.

Cover Design by: Mel Hearts

ISBN 978-1-0691211-1-0 paperback

ISBN 978-1-0691211-0-3 eBook

Dedication:

To our Lord Jesus Christ who blessed us with

The Journey of a Lifetime

To our sons and spouses:

David & Susan, Fr. Rick, Wayne & Kathie, Gerry & Barbara

To our Grandchildren:

Jennifer (David), Amanda (Chris), Sarah (John), Jonathon (Dani), Lauren (Josh), Emma (Haeden), Sarah (Aaron), Wayne (Brittany), Alexa (Jeremiah)

To our Great-Grandchildren:

Elijah, Cecilia, Audrey, Owen, Heidi, Cooper, Logan, Walker, Waylon, & Micah on the way

Acknowledgments

Special thanks to the many who have encouraged us to write this book especially David and Susan who also assisted us in editing the manuscript.

FAITH, FAMILY, AND FORTITUDE

The Journey of a Lifetime

In the Beginning.......

RICHARD

My grandparents from my mother's side came to Canada from Europe, the area of Poland and Ukraine. It was under the Austrian government at the time. My mother was two years old when they immigrated. My grandparents on my father's side also came to Canada about the same time. My father was five years old.

They lived in an area of Winnipeg called Fort Rouge. At the age of 27, my father, Joseph, married my mother, Mary. My father worked as a welder. At that time, jobs in Winnipeg were scarce, so my father purchased a farm in Gimli. My grandpa, on my father's side, Theodore, had also purchased a farm in that location.

There were five of us siblings in our family, four boys

and one girl. I was the fifth child. I would kid around and say that we were born at a very young age.

From Snowy Trails to Cod Liver Oil: Childhood Memories

When I was young, we would walk to school, which was 2 ¼ miles from our home. The journey was mostly through bushland. At the age of 8, I had to make this walk alone. It was often frightening because there were horses running loose in the bush, and cows and bulls grazing in the area.

Whenever I heard the horses running towards me, I would quickly climb a tree, even if it didn't have any branches. Initially, I wasn't afraid because I had my brother and sister walking with me. However, after they moved to a different school, I had to walk alone through the bush every day.

During winter, the snow in the bushes was quite deep. I took two pieces of 1x6 board, each 8 feet long, rounded the tips, soaked them in hot water, and bent them to create ski-like ends. I added straps for my footwear, and this is how I traversed the deep snow on my way to school.

Every morning before school, our routine included my mother giving us a tablespoon of cod liver oil, followed by an orange wedge to help with the taste. When we fell ill, antibiotics weren't an option. Instead, our mother would administer a tablespoon of castor oil. For more serious illnesses, the remedy involved a hot water bottle and a long hose (you can guess what that means.)

Farm Life: Joys and Solitude

Living on the farm was a happy time but also a lonely time. Our nearest neighbor was ½ mile away and the town was 6 miles away.

As a child, we didn't really have any toys to play with. I would invent my own toys. I remember using a clothes iron as a little car on the ground.

In the meadow near our home, deep banks of snow would gather on top of the ice. I built myself a little fort, an igloo, there. One day, as I crawled through the entrance, the igloo caved in on me, pinning me to the ice. It was hard to breathe and even harder to work my way out, especially since the igloo was built on top of the ice. Fortunately, I managed to free myself, as there was no one around to help me.

Springtime was always a wonderful season. We would watch as a huge caterpillar machine came down the road, clearing the deep snowbanks. With the snow cleared, traveling to town became much easier.

My father built a caboose for our winter trips to town for supplies. It was constructed on a sleigh and had a small wood stove inside for warmth. The frame was covered in felt paper. We would ride in it to town once a week. During the summer, we traveled by horse and buggy.

A Silver Spoon and Penicillin: My Recovery Story

One day, my sister and I were playing doctor, and she gave me several aspirins. When my mother found out, she asked me to kneel before a picture of Jesus in our home and pray for my well-being. I prayed, and thankfully, I didn't experience any adverse effects from the aspirins.

Our family would gather every evening kneeling around a bed and pray the Rosary.

When I was 9 years old, I had a severe stomach-ache at school. The teacher sent me home alone, walking the 2 ¼ miles by myself. As I trudged through the snow, I had to stop frequently and lie down because of the intense pain. The pain persisted overnight, so the next day, my parents took me to the hospital in Gimli by horse and sleigh. The doctor diagnosed me with a ruptured appendix. After the surgery, I developed a severe infection. The Benedictine nuns who ran the hospital and served as nurses gave me penicillin injections four times a day. I ended up with 42 needle marks on my arms. After about ten days, I recovered. The nuns said I must have been born with a silver spoon in my mouth because they were unsure if I would survive, given how sick I was.

My Favorite Gray Chicken: A Bittersweet Memory

I had a favorite gray chicken which I would often pat, and she would cackle as if she enjoyed this. One time I hadn't seen this chicken for a while, and I asked my mother where this chicken disappeared to. She said we ate it three weeks ago.

I didn't realize until later in life that my parents had not been well off. Living on the farm, we always had food on the table. Sometimes, we would have bread with jam cut into small squares, placed in a bowl like cereal, and eaten with milk. I thought it was a special treat, but years later, my parents told me that they didn't have cereal too often, and that's why we had this so-called treat.

We had several milking cows, four horses for pulling farm machinery, and lots of chickens. We used a hand-cranked separator to separate the cream from the milk. Every week, a local dairy truck would come to pick up the cream, and my parents would receive payment for it.

Weekly, my parents would take a crate of 30 dozen eggs to town and trade them for flour, sugar and other groceries. This was a time when farmers would gather in the store and visit with one another.

Farming was tough in those days. My father would walk mostly all day driving the horses and walking behind the machinery. He would take a gallon of water with him and drink it all as he worked.

The Wandering Wedding Ring: A Family Tale

My parents, Joseph and Mary, were married for 64 years. As my father was working on the farm, he lost his wedding ring. A few years later, while working in the garden, my mother found the lost ring with a cornstalk growing through it. Before their 50th anniversary, my father lost the ring again. He wished that he had the original ring, but he had to buy another one for the celebration. After selling the farm, they visited the new owner, who asked if my father had lost a ring. He had found it on the blade of the cultivator while working the land.

From Skunks to Apple Pies: Farm Life Stories

Our farm was relatively small by today's standards. We had a dry well in our yard, about 15 feet deep. One day we found that a skunk was in the well. My brother, Tony, took a .22 rifle, shot the skunk, and then asked our brother, Frank, to use a ladder to retrieve it. As Frank started down the ladder, another skunk emerged from the hole at the bottom. Frank quickly climbed out, luckily avoiding getting sprayed.

One of my chores, besides milking the cows, was to bring them home from the bush every day for milking time. I was always fearful of encountering the horses in the bush, especially one with an angry personality that scared me. This horse even bit my brother once, leaving teeth marks on his chest. Other chores included picking roots and stooking grain for the harvest. We also had a huge vegetable garden that my mother tended. On summer weekends, we would pick vegetables, strawberries, and raspberries, then take them to town to sell to the campers with cottages by the lake. These were my first experiences as a salesperson, and I usually sold everything within an hour.

On Sundays, we would often look up the road to see if anybody was coming from Winnipeg to visit. There were no phones at that time, so any visit was a surprise. Relatives visiting would always bring many treats. It was a such a happy time for all of us. When the guests drove into our yard the chickens would run, as before you knew it, my mother would have two chickens on the table to serve to the visitors.

We would go hunting for partridges and rabbits. My mother would cook them, and they were exceptionally delicious.

We had a neighbor who enjoyed hunting, and sometimes we would go hunting rabbits and partridges together. He was a war veteran and deaf in one ear, so he couldn't tell from which side the partridges were making noise.

Walter, another neighbor, also liked to hunt. I went hunting with him once. We were walking down a path in the bush, with him behind me. His rifle was an automatic .22 caliber. He accidentally pressed the trigger with the safety off, and a couple of shots whizzed by me. Fortunately, I wasn't hit. I never went hunting with him again.

I was a little entrepreneur setting traps on my way to school, catching rabbits and squirrels and weasels. I would skin them and ship the furs to Sydney I. Robinson in Winnipeg. I would get a cheque back in the mail; $0.05 for a rabbit fur, $1.50 for a squirrel and $4.50 for a weasel.

My mother would travel to Winnipeg by train a

couple of times a year to visit her family and buy clothing or other necessities. While she was away, my father took over the cooking. I remember him trying to make an apple pie once. He must have added yeast to the recipe because the pie ended up as tall as a loaf of bread, with just a little bit of apple in the middle.

First Confession: Three Pages of Sins

Once a month, the Catholic priest would visit our little church, which was 1 ¾ miles from home. He would preside at a Eucharistic Celebration at 4:00 p.m. on Sunday afternoons. Back then, we would fast from midnight to receive Holy Communion. We would eat only after walking back home, and by then, we were very, very hungry.

I remember going to confession for the first time. I prepared for days and had three full pages of sins to tell the priest. The confession took place in the sacristy. After confessing, reading the pages, I was ready to put the papers in my pocket. The priest asked me to give him the papers and he burned them in the little stove. I often wondered what those pages of sins were because I was only seven years old.

Ice Cream and Kindness: The Benedictine Nun

When I was 13 years old, my parents sent me to Winnipeg to attend St. Paul's High School. I lived right at the school as a boarder. As I look back it would have been quite expensive for them to do that.

Having never been away from home, I felt quite lonely. Every Friday after classes, I would catch a bus to the outskirts of Winnipeg and then hitchhike the sixty miles home. Sometimes, I was lucky and got a ride quickly, but other times, it took four or five rides to make it home.

One time I got as far as 1 ¾ miles from home and had to walk the rest of the way in a severe thunderstorm. The road was completely lit up by lightning. It was 1:00 a.m. when I finally reached home, but the door was locked. My parents were hesitant to open it at that hour because they thought it might be our alcoholic neighbor who sometimes came around at night. Eventually, they realized it was me and let me in.

At the time of attending St. Paul's High School, most

of the students had plenty of spending money. My parents, as I mentioned, were not well off so I did not have an allowance. To have a little spending money, I worked in the kitchen washing dishes daily. The Benedictine nuns ran the kitchen. One nun was very kind to me. She would give me a huge bowl of ice cream, five scoops, any day I wanted it which was almost every day.

From Mischief to Maturity: Life Under Jesuit Discipline

On Friday nights, many students would go out to the movies as it was our night out, with a curfew of 10:30. I couldn't afford the ticket price, so two of my friends and I would sneak into the theater. We would wait by the exit door and slip in when someone left. Occasionally, we got caught and had to leave.

The Jesuit priests ran the school and were quite strict with discipline. If I misbehaved, I was sent to the prefect's office, where the usual punishment was a strap on the palms of my hands. One time, while walking down the hallway in the residence, a priest asked me, "What are you doing?" I sarcastically replied,

"Nothing." As a result, I was punished by not being allowed to leave the premises for a month—no movies, no going home, nothing.

Another time, I came in later than the curfew and tried to sneak into the dormitory. The hallways were pitch black, and as I turned a corner, this priest who was about seven feet tall appeared out of the dark and caught me in a headlock. He scared the daylights out of me, and I don't remember ever being late after that. He was stern, but you knew he cared for you and your welfare. He had a twinkle in his eye, and I liked him. I admired many of the priests who taught us. They maintained good order but also genuinely cared about the students. They were like substitutes for our parents while we lived away from home.

All in all, this was a good school of really dedicated priests running it and a very good experience as a student. I served Mass daily in the chapel.

Smoke and Mirrors: Outwitting the Principal

After attending St. Paul's for grades 9 and 10, I returned to Gimli High School for grades 11 and 12 because the overall cost was too much for my parents.

A few of us students were quite mischievous. There was a room in the school's basement where the coal for the furnace was stored, and several of us would sneak in there to smoke during recess. One day, while we were in that room, the principal came into the basement. Smelling the smoke, he wanted to check out the room but didn't have his keys. He sent a student to his office to fetch them. Before the student returned, he came around to the outside window and warned us that the principal was at the door and about to catch us smoking. We quickly escaped through the window and went to the basement and watched as the principal, smiling, thought he was about to make a big catch. The principal opened the door only to find that we had already escaped. He was certainly angry that we had outsmarted him.

We did several pranks but dreaded getting caught as the principle would tell us to go home and bring back our father. I was afraid to ask my father to come to school with me as he would get quite angry with me.

Dust and Danger: A Noon Hour Adventure

During a noon hour break at school, a student, Robert asked a few of us if we wanted to go for a ride with him. He had brought his parents' car to school. We agreed, and soon found ourselves speeding down a loose gravel road, kicking up a huge cloud of dust as we hit 100 miles per hour. Suddenly, a large dog appeared from behind a hay rack on the same road. Our car hit the dog, causing the entire vehicle to tilt to one side. We thought we were going to roll over. After that terrifying experience, we never went for another ride with Robert. I really believe that God protected us that day from what could have been a disaster.

Snowstorm Survival: A Walk to Remember

Gimli High School was about 6 miles from home. My brother Frank worked at the airport, which was 4 miles away, so I rode with him each day. From there, I took a bus for the remaining 2 miles to school. One day, we faced a huge blizzard and had to walk 4 miles as the road was completely impassable. With near-zero visibility, we followed a fence to stay on track. After a couple of miles, my brother wanted to lie down in the snow to rest. I insisted we keep moving, knowing that stopping could mean falling asleep and never waking up. We continued walking until we reached a neighbor's place, three-quarters of a mile from home. After resting there for a while, we finally made it home. Our parents had been very worried and had prayed for our safe return.

NATALIE

From Ukraine to Canada: A Family Story

My grandparents, Dora and Anton Semenkiw (though everyone called them Semeniuk), emigrated from Zalicia, a village in the province of Borschiw, Ukraine, on May 10, 1903. They settled north of Dauphin, Manitoba, where they worked tirelessly on their farm. They were devout people, and my grandfather even helped build the Ukrainian Catholic Church in Pulp River. They had 12 children, with my mom being the youngest. While some of their children were born in Ukraine, my mom was born on the farm in Canada.

I was born in Ethelbert, Manitoba. I never knew my

father. When I was a toddler, my mom married my stepfather, who worked on the Algoma Central Railway, which ran north of Sault Ste. Marie, Ontario. He was a section foreman in Scully, just north of Franz, Ontario. Franz was a very, very small town where the Algoma Central Railway crossed the Canadian Pacific Railway. Mom and I lived in Scully until I was of school age, after which my stepfather built a home for us in Franz.

From Scalding Pain to Chick Comfort

Around the age of four, I woke up one morning and went straight to my potty. Mom had just taken a pan of boiling water off the stove and placed it on a bench, under which my potty was located. When I sat down, I accidentally tipped the pan over. The worst burns were on my left shoulder, with splashes on my face, arm, and foot. There was no immediate train to take me to a hospital in Sault Ste. Marie, so we didn't get there until the next day.

I woke up in the hospital inside a tent made of white sheets with bright lights inside this tent. My left arm was wrapped in white gauze and suspended in the air. It was a frightening experience. I cried a lot. So much so, that my mother asked if she could take me home. The hospital agreed, but she had to sign a form releasing them from responsibility if anything went wrong.

It felt so good being home and Mom made my day. A shipment of baby chicks arrived. She brought them into the house and let them loose by my bed. She knew that I often spent hours in the chicken coop watching the chickens. I loved watching these baby chicks and holding some of them. This was a huge help in the healing process.

Blueberries, Bears, and Bush Hides

We would go to Franz to buy groceries and mingle with friends. My stepfather would head to the hotel to drink beer and gamble with his friends, while Mom and I shopped at the two grocery stores. One time, as the stores were closing, Mom went to the hotel to tell my stepfather it was time to go home. He became furious. When we got home, he was yelling at Mom. He went upstairs, grabbed my toy trunk, and threw it down the stairs at us. Mom quickly grabbed me, and we ran outside into the bush.

We could hear my stepfather yelling her name. She was afraid, and we tried to stay very quiet. We kept moving through the bush until we came to an abandoned shack where we spent the night. The next morning, we heard him calling for Mom, but we stayed hidden. Eventually, we heard him head towards Franz in his railway motor car, probably thinking we had gone there. Mom decided it was safe to go home then.

This episode left a lasting impact on me. As an adult, any stress or anxiety would make my whole body shake. This continued until one day, friends from a prayer group prayed for me specifically about this issue.

This was the only episode of violence I remember. Despite this, I was happy living in the wilderness. I often jumped from rock to rock on the edge of a lake just across from our home in Scully. I had no siblings, but there were Indigenous families living by the lake, and their children were my playmates.

Sometimes, as a family, we went fishing. There's nothing like fresh-caught pickerel cooked over an open fire.

Mom loved picking blueberries, though I wasn't as enthusiastic. Blueberries grew abundantly around our home in Scully. She would grab a pot and spoon to bang on in case a black bear appeared, and off she'd go. She even earned some money by selling baskets of blueberries to the men working on the passing trains. We also enjoyed wild strawberries and raspberries. It was fortunate that nature provided all this for us because we had no electricity, making it difficult to keep things fresh. Our summer fridge was a dugout in the side of a hill by our house.

To mail a letter, we would wave a flag, and the engineer would slow the train. One of the railway cars would have its door open. Mom would wedge the letter into a slit in a stick and throw it through the open door as the train went by slowly.

Courage and Catechism: A Childhood Memory

There was a Roman Catholic church in Franz, Ontario,

but the priest could only visit occasionally. Looking back on my life, I can see how God was drawing me to Him, even in my childhood. I remember a nun coming to our town in the summer to teach us catechism. One day, she told us that in some countries, people can't go to church openly and might even be shot for their faith. She asked us, "What would you do if someone came through that door with a gun and asked you to stand up if you believed in Jesus?" I remember going home, wanting to be the person who would stand up and say, "Yes," but wondering if I would have the courage.

Running from the Past: A New Life in Winnipeg

All this time, I thought my stepfather was my father. Around the age of 12, Mom asked a friend to explain to me that he was not my father. He rambled on and on, and I didn't get the message. A few days later, Mom told me in plain words. I didn't feel much because my stepfather was distant, and we had no real relationship.

Shortly after, Mom left him. Every year, she would visit Grandpa and Grandma and her sister's family in Pulp River, later Pine River. My stepfather thought we were going for another visit, just before I was to start Grade 9.

Mom didn't want my stepfather to know where we lived in Winnipeg. But somehow, he found out I worked part-time at the Beacon Theatre while going to school. One evening, he showed up and said he was coming with me after work to see where we lived. He told me he would not come in. I thought of Mom's friend living quite close to us on Selkirk Avenue. I pretended that was where we lived. When the bus passed by our friend's house, I got off, went around the back of the house, and ran down some back lanes as quietly as I could, in case he got off and followed me. It worked!

When we first came to Winnipeg, Mom found a job, but we had very little money. We rented one room on the second floor of a home on Alfred Ave. God took care of us. We went to see a movie on Main Street, and they happened to be giving away prizes that night. We won a small set of dishes, which meant we could prepare something to eat. We were so happy with a toaster, a hot plate, and now a set of dishes.

RICHARD

From Shovels to Sales: Early Job Adventures

After high school, I moved to Winnipeg and lived with my Uncle Joe and Aunt Nellie, who had five children at home. My first job was digging with a shovel for an underpass from a parking lot to the Eaton's store for two days. Over time, I had several jobs. I enjoyed working as an advertising representative for Canada Packers, setting up displays in grocery stores. Later, I became a salesperson for another packing house, calling on grocery stores. I still remember one restaurant in downtown Winnipeg that would buy rolls of ham when they were already green and offered ham and eggs for just 99 cents.

I remember learning how to roller skate and spotting a nice-looking girl sitting on a bench across the rink. I sped across the rink but couldn't stop, crashed into the wall, and fell. After getting up, I asked her, "Would you like to skate with me?" She replied, "No thank you."

At that time, I owned a 1949 Austin A40 with a stick

shift. One day, while driving down the street, my brakes failed. I had to gear down to try and slow the car. I ended up driving onto the sidewalk. My cousin Stan, who was with me, asked, "Why are you driving on the sidewalk?" I replied, "I'm trying to slow down because the brakes failed, and I can't stop."

The Girl with the Blue Eyes: A Love Story

I had heard that Imperial Tobacco was a good company to work for, so I called them to inquire about any openings for a salesman. Although they initially said there were no openings, they called me back a few days later for an interview. I got the job and became a traveling salesman for the company, selling tobacco, cigarettes, cigars, and pipe tobacco to stores all over Winnipeg. I received a good salary and a brand-new company car.

It was New Year's Eve, and a friend and I went to a dance. There, I saw a beautiful girl sitting with a guy, and I was immediately attracted to her. I approached her and asked if she would like to dance with me. She looked at me with her beautiful blue eyes and said, "No thanks." Her name was Natalie.

At the time, Natalie worked as a secretary at Air Canada and taught accordion part-time at a music studio. I knew one of the guys who worked at the same studio, and one weekend while I was visiting my parents in Gimli, he decided to come out and brought Natalie with him. This was my big chance to make a move, and I did. I got Natalie's phone number, called her, and we started dating in August of 1959.

On Friday, November 13th of that year, I told Natalie

I wanted to stop by St. John Cantius Church to see my brother, who was a pastor there. Inside the church, I took out a ring I had purchased and asked her to marry me. Without hesitation, she said, "Yes." We saw each other daily until we got married on May 14th, 1960. It was a whirlwind romance filled with love.

Shortly after we were married, Imperial Tobacco transferred me to Saskatoon, Saskatchewan. My sales territory covered a quarter of the province, from Saskatoon to Prince Albert to Lloydminster, Alberta. On Sunday nights, I would pack my bag and be gone from Monday until Friday, returning home for the weekends. I traveled about 300 miles a day, visiting 30 stores. During this time, our first son, David, was born, and I didn't like being away from home so much. I decided to quit my job and started working for a finance company, where my job involved chasing down customers who didn't pay their bills.

There was someone assigned to train me for this job. On my first day, he said, "We're going 20 miles out of town to a farmer who hasn't paid for his furniture. We're either going to collect the money owed or repossess the furniture." We had a large moving truck following us to load up the furniture. When we arrived, the farmer was furious, wielding a huge butcher knife, swinging it in the air, and cursing. I thought, "What have I gotten myself into? I could lose my life over this job." We ran back to our car and let the movers repossess the furniture.

Starting Fresh: Launching My Own Insurance Agency

A couple of years earlier, I had applied for a job in Winnipeg as an insurance agent with Allstate. Natalie and I were thrilled when the manager called, asking if we would like to move back to Winnipeg and work for Allstate. They even covered all our moving expenses. We jumped at the chance and couldn't say "YES" loud enough.

At this time our second son, Rick was born.

I worked at Allstate for three years and really enjoyed it. My boss was fantastic and a super salesman. One day he made a wager bet with us that the next person who came in to pay a bill would leave with a life insurance policy. A 72-year-old man walked in and, sure enough, he left with a life insurance policy.

Allstate had a nationwide contest called Black Friday, held during a week with Friday the 13th. They offered many prizes for different policies sold. I ended up winning all the prizes for Canada, including a camera, Corning Ware, and an all-expenses-paid trip to Florida. That week, I sold 20 life insurance policies.

I decided to start my own insurance agency and signed agreements with several insurance companies to represent them. I rented a beautiful new office with my high school friend Tom, an accountant. Additionally, I ventured into the real estate business.

During this period, our third son, Wayne, and our fourth son, Gerry, were born. I vividly remember the doctor coming out after each birth with a big grin on his face, announcing, "It's another boy." Four boys in total.

A Home Full of Music and Love

In 1966, we bought our first home on Renfrew St. It was a 1,148 square foot bungalow with three bedrooms, a living and dining room, a full basement with a recreational room, and a two-car garage. Our home was just half a block from St. John Brebeuf, the Catholic church and school where we attended Mass, and the boys went to school. One time, we were running late, so we all hopped in the car and drove the half block to church, only to find no parking spaces. We ended up parking back in front of our house.

Our home was a gathering place for the many friends of our boys. They would bring them over to play games, ping pong, pool, sports, etc. Our boys had also started a band, practicing in our home with friends. David and Rick took guitar lessons, David on guitar and Rick on bass. Wayne took drum lessons. For a short time, Gerry tried the accordion. I remember them playing at a high school event one time and I went to hear them. The auditorium was full, and girls were just screaming as they played. Our boys were like Rock Stars.

These were truly joyful times. While some people couldn't wait for their children to leave home, we felt the opposite, wishing they could stay with us forever.

David began playing every Sunday night at St. Ignatius Church for the 9:00 p.m. evening Mass, which was always packed with young people. Each of our boys excelled in their studies, consistently ranking at the top of their classes and receiving numerous awards. They were responsible and well-behaved, often working at Dutch Maid, a restaurant and ice cream store, as teenagers to contribute significantly towards their education. We felt truly blessed that they never got involved in drugs, alcohol, or bad behavior.

They later attended St. Paul's High School and then St. Paul's at the University of Manitoba, as we believed a Catholic education was very important.

NATALIE

Love, Laughter, and Music: Our Family's Tale

As I mentioned, I didn't know a father's love, but God blessed me with a loving, warm-hearted, and fun-loving husband, Richard, and four wonderful sons. Richard is my soulmate. At the time of writing this book, we have been married for 64 years, and if I could do it all over again, I wouldn't hesitate.

I remember waking up on our wedding day and literally Spring had arrived that day. The leaves had come out overnight and everything was green and beautiful. It was almost like a sign of a wonderful new beginning.

It was thrilling to play house for real. In that first week of marriage, I was ironing Richard's shirt and loving it. As a young married couple with four little ones, we didn't have much money. I sewed covers for wooden orange crates to use as end tables by their beds. It didn't matter; we were just happy to be together.

Our children were our delight. How we loved seeing things through their eyes when we went on trips. They would put on puppet shows in our backyard for the neighborhood kids. When they were older, their band practiced in our home, and the walls reverberated with the beat of the music. I relished every moment! Our home was filled with love and laughter.

Our home became the place for family gatherings and the start of a new tradition. When Richard was growing up, his mother always made carrot pie, not pumpkin pie, for Thanksgiving. His father's birthday was around Thanksgiving, so instead of a cake, I would put candles on a carrot pie.

RICHARD

A Bold Faith: How One Visit Changed My Life

One day in 1974, a fellow I knew and admired for his business ethics in real estate, who was also a devout Catholic, visited us. He wanted to share his experience of a new relationship with Jesus. He spoke for about two hours, and all the while, I was thinking I wished we could talk about business instead of spiritual matters. However, his boldness in sharing his faith left an impression on us.

About a year later, he came to visit us again. I wasn't too eager to spend another two hours and even considered pretending we weren't home. But I thought he might have seen some movement in the house, so we decided to open the door. Once again, he shared his faith with us for a long time.

At that time, my sole objective in life seemed to be making money. I was successful in business and made good money. I used to think that if I had $5,000 in the bank and a paid-off house, I would really be happy. Well, I achieved both, but something was still missing.

The problem with money is that we think we own it, but if we're not careful, it ends up owning us. A father once said to his son, "Don't you want to succeed in life as I did?" The son replied, "Well, I don't know. You were raised in the country and worked hard to move to the city. You became a slave to own a house in the city and almost killed yourself to buy this house in the country. I think I'm better off staying here than making that wrong trip."

Another fellow wrote, "For years, I pretended to love my rich aunt's cats so she would remember me in her will. It worked! When she died, she left me the cats."

A Hundred Steps to Heaven: Our Spiritual Transformation

I attended Mass every Sunday, but I found it boring and often daydreamed during the service. To me, Jesus was someone who lived 2,000 years ago, and maybe if I was good, I would see Him when I died. I certainly didn't feel He was alive or present today.

Natalie and I had a conversation about life in general. We both felt there had to be more to life than just making money. When this Realtor invited us to a Full Gospel Businessmen's Breakfast at the Ramada Inn, we immediately said, "Yes."

We went and saw about 200 people. There was something different about them. There was a lot of joy in the room. We sat down at a table with three other couples. We had our breakfast and then there was singing and praising the Lord. Well, we got goosebumps. We had never heard anyone sing and praise the Lord like that. These people **really** loved the Lord.

Then one of the fellows at our table, whom we had

been talking to, stood up and said he had a vision of Jesus with his arms outstretched to everyone in the room. I leaned over to Natalie and said, "This man is crazy." We had never heard of visions before this.

We stayed and heard a man give his testimony of how he had come to know the Lord. We were excited hearing about Jesus. We wanted to know Jesus like that man. We wanted to see Jesus working in our life every day like he did.

We went to many of these breakfasts to hear speakers share how Jesus had touched their lives. At one of them, there was an invitation for people to come forward to invite Jesus into their lives and experience Him personally. Our son, Rick was with us, and we went up as a family, and from that moment, we truly started to experience God in our lives. It was just a simple prayer, but it felt like we took one step toward Jesus, and He took a hundred steps toward us.

Then someone told us about a weekly prayer meeting at a Catholic church, something we didn't know existed. We began attending and participated in a Life in the Spirit Seminar. After the community prayed over us with the laying on of hands for the full release of the Holy Spirit in our lives in February 1976, the following days felt like a small taste of heaven. It was a powerful experience.

The Life in the Spirit Seminars are designed as an introduction to a life lived in the power of the Holy Spirit. They provide an opportunity for people to find out more about that life, and to be helped in taking the first steps of a new relationship with the Lord.

A Spiritual Awakening: From Routine to Revival

After we had committed our lives to the Lord, we were so excited. The Bible came so alive, like it was a personal letter written to me. My parents were already elderly, and I would bring my Bible to them and show them passages that were speaking to my heart. They probably were wondering, what's happened to our youngest son. We of course told them, and my mother, soon after, took a Life in the Spirit Seminar and started to attend weekly prayer meetings. It was Pentecost over and over again, as we saw multitudes coming to Jesus and receiving the Holy Spirit. The prayer group grew to over 400 attending every Friday evening. Later, some members moved and started groups in their own parishes, so the attendance dropped to about 250 weekly.

I asked the Lord to forgive me for all the sins I had committed. When I randomly opened my Bible, my eyes fell on the words: *"Remember this, O Jacob, you O Israel, who are my servant! I formed you to be a servant to me; O Israel, by me you shall never be forgotten I have brushed away your offenses like a cloud, your sins like a mist."* (Isaiah 44:21-22)

The next day, we were at my brother Tony's place, and he said, "I have a Scripture passage I think the Lord wants me to give you." It was the same passage: *"Remember this, O Jacob... I have brushed away your offenses..."*—just in case I didn't get it the first time.

I could sense Jesus so close and found that I now had a whole new, exciting life. Before this experience, every time I went to the Sacrament of Reconciliation, it felt like I could have just photocopied my sins and handed them to the priest, saying, "Here it is, I did it again." Now, my list of sins was much shorter.

I went to Mass as usual the next Sunday, and when our pastor gave his sermon, I wondered what had happened to him. After Mass, I told him, "Father, that was the best sermon I've heard in this church in 10 years." He thanked me, probably puzzled by my comment.

The following Sunday, the associate pastor gave the homily. I usually found it hard to concentrate when he spoke, but this time, his words were alive. I couldn't believe my ears. After the service, I told him what a good homily he had given. I thought he had really changed.

On the way to the car, I realized what had happened. It wasn't the pastors who had changed; God had changed me. My ears were open, I was spiritually alive, and my life was no longer empty.

Do you want an exciting life? All you need to do is surrender to the Lord and watch him in action in your life.

We were asked to join the prayer teams to pray for people after the meetings. The first time we did this, an 18-year-old young lady came in for prayer. As we placed our hands on her shoulder, she slumped to the floor, a phenomenon known as resting in the Spirit. Natalie and I looked at each other, unsure of what to do next, as she was overwhelmed by the presence of the Holy Spirit.

We were later asked if we would lead the healing teams every Friday night. There were 52 people praying in 10 different rooms of 5 each. Many people would come for prayer support for their needs.

NATALIE

Heaven Insurance: A Life-Changing Faith Experience

I don't know where our four sons, Richard, and I would be today in our faith journey if we hadn't been touched through the Charismatic Renewal. We attended church every Sunday, taught our sons their evening prayers, and sent them to parochial schools from the start. I believed there was a God. I believed Jesus was the Son of God. I believed in eternal life, but I didn't experience God walking beside me daily or have conversations with Him.

But, oh how God moved in our lives when we took

one extra step toward Him! We had heard that if you go to Mass and receive Holy Communion on the first Friday of the month for nine months, you would die in a state of grace. One day, Richard said, "Let's get some heaven insurance." So, on the first Friday of September 1975, we went to Mass. Just a week later, we received a phone call from the Realtor inviting us to a breakfast, which eventually led us to participate in a Life in the Spirit Seminar. This was the life-changing experience of our lives.

I felt an overwhelming physical sensation of joy in my heart, so much so that I thought I couldn't take any more. That was my honeymoon period with the Lord.

After this experience, the Mass came alive for me. I kept noticing things in the Missal that I hadn't seen before. The words "Holy Spirit" became special, no longer just words but a person—God. I realized how often the Holy Spirit is mentioned in the Mass.

The Bible's words also became alive and meaningful. To this day, God keeps a hunger in my heart for reading the Scriptures.

We began praying and reading Scripture together as a

family after supper. Sometimes this led to discussions, and other times it was just intercessory prayer. We always shared with our family what we witnessed at prayer meetings and conferences. We saw God moving in powerful ways—the blind could see, the deaf could hear, the lame could walk, even getting out of wheelchairs. These were things we thought only happened when Jesus walked the earth. Our sons also saw God keep His promise to be with us in our trials.

A Journey of Healing: From Shyness to Strength

I think I was the shyest person on earth. I would never, never have stood in front of a group to give a talk, not even for a million dollars. On my first date, I was so afraid to speak that I barely said a word all evening. It's no wonder I never heard from that fellow again.

The first time I was asked to lead a prayer meeting, I thought, "I don't know if I can do this." I immediately turned to the Lord and asked for a Scripture reading. I opened to the passage where Jesus asked Simon Peter if he loved Him and then said, *"Feed my lambs, tend my sheep, and feed my sheep."* (John 21) I knew then that He was asking me to lead the prayer meeting, and I had to trust that the Lord would see me through it.

After the seminar, the Holy Spirit was the power healing and changing me. So much so, that God has used me to give many talks. Early on, a participant at a prayer meeting said he saw fire coming out of my mouth. That was an encouraging word from the Lord.

Fr. Hampsch

In this new life, the Lord leads us as a shepherd leads his sheep. An example of this in my life was when Richard and I were holidaying in California. One evening, we attended a prayer meeting in Escondido, where they announced an upcoming event with Fr. Hampsch, who would conduct a "Healing of Memories" session. It was going to be about five hours long. We thought, "Five hours? No way, that's too long and probably boring." So, we didn't pay attention to the details.

A few days later, we were in San Diego. After a day of shopping and sightseeing, we stopped for dinner. While eating, we looked through a directory of prayer groups and saw a meeting listed for that evening. We called to check if it was still on. The person said no but asked where we were.

"Well, as a matter of fact, there is a meeting tonight just a couple of blocks from where you are," they said. We went. It was Fr. Hampsch. Those five hours were like one, and that night, I felt just like I did when I was prayed over for the full release of the Holy Spirit. I was healed of something. To this day, I don't know what it was, but I felt freer.

Silent Prayer and Safe Rides

When Rick was a teenager, he had no intention of

becoming a priest. In fact, he graduated with a Masters in Statistics.

However, we discovered quite by accident that he was a prayerful teenager. One summer, his brother David would take Rick to work on Richard's motorcycle. One morning, they were riding down Taylor Ave when a car pulled out from the Reh-Fit Centre right in front of them.

They pictured themselves flying over the car and getting badly injured. As David applied the brakes, they skidded sideways and just clipped the front fender of the car with the bike's roll bar. The Autopac adjuster told Richard that it's very unusual to have a motorcycle accident without any injury.

Rick told us he knew why. Every morning, while sitting on the back of the motorcycle, he would silently pray the Rosary on a Rosary ring that he wore.

From Prayer Corner to Priesthood: Rick's Calling

When Rick graduated from the University of Manitoba, he went to work for the government in Ottawa. Notice how the Lord leads, Rick happened to find an apartment just a couple of blocks away from the only youth prayer group in Ottawa, which he joined and later led.

One Christmas, when he came home, he watched a video teaching by Fr. John Bertolucci, who suggested creating a small prayer corner in your room. He recommended placing a cloth on a little table, adding a candle and a holy picture, and spending an hour there every day.

Rick followed this advice, and three months later, he called us and said, "I think God is calling me to change my vocation. I think He's calling me to be a priest." Although Rick had always been prayerful, this intensified period of prayer helped him hear the call.

Msgr. Stan, Richard's brother, was a pastor in Brandon, Manitoba and he didn't come to Winnipeg very often. Rick asked the Lord to confirm his call to the priesthood by having Msgr. Stan in Winnipeg for Wayne's birthday. And he was!

During these three months, someone Rick barely knew from church offered him a ride home and asked if he had ever thought about becoming a priest. At the same time, the Companions of the Cross, a group of young men including Rick, were just starting to meet with Fr. Bob Bedard. They also confirmed his calling.

When Rick was ordained, something struck me. Around the time Richard and I were baptized in the Holy Spirit in 1976, someone shared a Scripture reading with us that stayed in our hearts. We didn't understand its meaning for us then, but we felt it was an important word from God. It was Isaiah 44:3-5: *"I will pour out my Spirit upon your offspring, and my blessing upon your descendants. They shall spring up amid the verdure like poplars beside the flowing waters. One shall say, 'I am the Lord's,' another shall be named after Jacob, and this one shall write on his hand, 'The Lord's,' and Israel shall be his surname."*

In 1990, that Scripture passage came to pass. Our third son, Wayne, became ill and died within six weeks, but he gave his life to the Lord, saying, "Whatever will be, will be." Isaiah 44: *One shall say, 'I am the Lord's.'*

Rick was not supposed to be ordained until June 1991, but Fr. Bob Bedard discerned with the bishop that he should be ordained sooner, six months earlier, on

December 15, 1990. When Rick was ordained, the bishop was generous with the oil, anointing Rick's hands to the point where they were almost dripping with oil. Isaiah 44: *And this one shall write on his hand, 'The Lord's.'*

Heavenly Signs in Our Darkest Hour: Wayne's Journey

In 1990, there was a meeting with prayer group leaders in Winnipeg. We broke into small groups to pray for one another. A lady praying with Richard and me felt the Lord saying, "Soon you will have many troubles, but know that I am with you." I wasn't concerned, thinking it would probably be another financial trial, something we had faced before with the Lord's help.

A month or so later, we attended another meeting in Calgary, Alberta, with leaders of prayer groups from Western Canada. During prayer, someone had an image of a volcanic mountain ready to explode and saw me like the Blessed Mother. We all know the agony the Blessed Mother endured. I didn't hear much else because my thoughts were fixated on the volcanic mountain, which didn't sound good!

The next morning, the lady who had prayed for us the evening before approached me at breakfast. She wanted to remind us of the Scripture reading she had for us during prayer, feeling strongly that we should hold onto it. It was Ephesians 6, which is all about the armor of God.

See how good God is. I did not hear that warning from the Lord because I was so hung up on the vision. The Lord nudged her to come and give us that warning again, reminding us to protect our faith by putting on the armor of God.

For two weeks, our 27-year-old son Wayne thought he had the flu. On March 19, 1990, he was diagnosed with acute myeloblastic leukemia (AML) and was immediately in critical condition in intensive care. It went through him like wildfire, and he passed away on May 3, 1990.

Wayne was a brilliant student. He had earned a master's degree in Astronomy from the University of Victoria and was working towards a PhD. His writings had disproved some long-held theory and are still taught in universities today. At the time he became ill, he had been married for seven months to a wonderful person named Kathie.

Wayne needed a bone marrow transplant, and his brothers were all perfect matches. However, he couldn't get to that point because he was in a germ-filled hospital environment without proper protection. For six weeks, he endured strong chemotherapy, which made even the touch of bed sheets painful. His wife Kathie stayed by his side, comforting him day after day.

Two and a half weeks before his death, the doctors told us that Wayne only had a 5% chance of survival and that his brain was damaged due to a fungal infection. This infection attacked him when his immunity was down to nothing because of the chemotherapy. It was as if he stroked four times in different parts of his brain.

When we received the news, I was physically shaking. But as we walked out into the hospital hallway, I suddenly experienced a profound peace, unlike anything I had ever felt before or since. It was an absolute stillness inside me, from head to toe, as if my entire body was silent. In this silence, I sensed the words, "It's O.K....... it's O.K." I knew it was God's presence.

I felt prompted to ask Richard, "How do you feel? I mean inside." He replied, "I feel peace." This sense of peace lasted about 15 minutes and was a precious gift from God because I can still recall it to this day.

During Wayne's hospital stay, I completed a novena to St. Therese and wondered how I would receive my rose this time. The next day, a woman called to say she had been praying for Wayne and had a vision of a white dove with a white rose in its beak.

I knew my novena had been heard and answered with a white rose, but I wondered why it was white instead of red. I later learned that white symbolizes resurrection, and in Europe, people sometimes place a white rose on a coffin. Someone else mentioned that when St. Therese answers with a white rose, it's the ultimate answer.

There were countless instances where God showed His presence. Our greatest consolation and comfort is knowing that Wayne is with God. On the very first day

Wayne was diagnosed and hospitalized, he was anointed by Msgr. Stan, Richard's brother, and God touched Wayne deeply. The next day, Wayne told his wife, Kathie, "I don't believe in eternal life, I **know** there is eternal life." Kathie replied, "Yes, I know." Wayne insisted, "No, Kathie, you don't understand. What happened yesterday was real." He added, "I'm glad it wasn't an accident and that I have time to prepare." I remember how happy he was when he said he gave his life to Jesus and accepted whatever would happen. He later told us, "Now I know what you've been talking about," referring to the experiences we had shared with him.

After the funeral, many people told us they felt Wayne was with God. But Richard and I needed direct consolation from God, so we prayed, "Lord, please don't be angry with us, but show us again. Let someone come to us and tell us that Wayne is with You."

The very next day, Fr. Driscoll, who had been at our church when the boys were in grade school and had served as altar boys for him, came over. He had been in

Florida the night Wayne was dying.   That night, Fr. Driscoll had a dream in which he felt compelled to write to Wayne and share the Mass readings for that day. He woke up, went back to sleep, and had the same dream again.   The next day, the message from the dreams stayed with him strongly.   The Scripture readings were about believing and the resurrection!

Adding to this, and what felt like icing on the cake from God, Fr. Driscoll wrote Wayne a letter, which he gave us when he visited. In it, he wrote, "You, Wayne, are not puzzled, you are not confused, your heart is not broken, you live, you know, you know Him and have seen Him. You know, we must believe."

This echoed exactly what Wayne had said after he was anointed: "I no longer believe; I know there's eternal life."

About a week and a half before Wayne's death, Richard and I were praying at home when Richard had a mental picture of one decade of the Rosary in gold. We wondered what it meant. The day after Wayne's death, on May 4th, we attended a Mass at St. Paul's High School which was offered for Wayne.   The celebrant mentioned, "This is the month of May, the month of Mary." A light bulb went on inside of me and I understood the vision. Wayne died on the first week of May, the month of Mary. Hebrews 12:22-23 speaks of the spirits of just men made perfect and dwelling in the City of Zion, the heavenly Jerusalem.

A few days before Wayne died, I was in our backyard, crying out to the Lord, "Do something." I had witnessed people being healed; why wasn't it happening now. In my heart, I felt God asking, "What was your job in raising the boys?" I thought, "To bring them to You." And the words came, "You've done it."

Later, Richard felt the Lord saying in prayer, "You have given the greatest gift of love to Wayne, the gift of eternal life." He felt this meant our teaching and telling Wayne about Jesus.

About half an hour before Wayne died, God, in His love and mercy, allowed us to witness something extraordinary. Wayne had been in a coma all night, with a blood pressure of 40 over 20, almost brain dead, and hadn't moved at all. But shortly before he died, he started to nod, making 6 or 7 definite "yes" nods. He was on a ventilator for the last three weeks, which had prevented him from nodding up or down, only sideways.

We asked the nurse what this was. We had an idea but wanted to ensure it wasn't a nerve reflex or something else. The nurse had never seen anything like it before. We asked our son Gerry, the doctor, and he said he had never heard of anything like it either. We had heard of Jesus or angelic beings coming for people at death. We believe Wayne was saying, "Yes, he's ready."

A month after Wayne died, we went to Morden, Manitoba, to help with a Life in the Spirit Seminar. After the prayer for baptism in the Holy Spirit, a small group also prayed for us. During this prayer, a lady shared a mental picture that came to her. She almost didn't share it because she didn't understand its meaning and had never experienced something like it before.

She saw a door with a window in the top part. Through the window, she saw a young man on the other side, smiling, very happy, with beautiful bright blue eyes, wearing a very white T-shirt. Wayne had blue eyes and always wore a T-shirt. That was Wayne!

God can give us insights into the spiritual realm. Shortly after his death, we wondered what Wayne was doing. That evening we were watching the evening news. They were talking about a tax on the sale of books, and they showed Wayne in a bookstore. We couldn't believe our eyes and made sure to watch the 11 o'clock news. We vaguely remembered Wayne mentioning a few months before his illness that he was in a bookstore while a news crew was filming. What did all this mean? We felt God was telling us that Wayne was learning.

Yes, we were shaken by this experience, but because of God, we have not been shattered. It makes a **huge** difference when you experience God in your life and know that he's around.

To this day, I say that God gave me a mink coat that year for Christmas. It wasn't something I longed for, but as a little girl, I thought if I ever had a fur coat, white mink would be nice, just like in the movies.

Just before Christmas, my cousin's wife, Mary Jane,

called me from Victoria, British Columbia. She said, "I hope you're not offended, but would you be interested in this fur coat I have?" It didn't fit her anymore, and she didn't need it in Victoria. She offered it to me for free. I said, "Sure," not expecting anything spectacular. When I received the parcel and opened it, I couldn't believe my eyes. It was gorgeous, the kind you see in movies—white mink with strips of black leather.

This was a gift from the Lord in the midst of our greatest sorrow, the first Christmas without Wayne. It was God's whisper of love, saying, "See, here is a special gift for you because I love you."

Even in death, God's glory can shine and impact others. Richard shared Wayne's faith with an orderly. The orderly said that he and his family didn't go to church, but he came to the funeral, something he ordinarily wouldn't do. Afterwards, he told us that he believes in eternal life and is rethinking and changing his priorities. Many of the nursing staff from Intensive Care came to the funeral. They said, "Now and then, a person comes through here and touches our lives, and Wayne is one of them."

RICHARD

God's Grace: Overcoming Prejudice and Unforgiveness

When I first started attending prayer meetings, I was in the real estate business. An elderly lady wanted to sell her home at what I thought was a bargain price. We decided to buy it, fix it up, and rent it out as an investment. Natalie, my parents, and I spent two months remodeling everything, turning it into a beautiful, upgraded home. We advertised it for rent, and a couple came to see it and decided to rent it. Without doing any background checks, we rented it to them. I planned to personally go to the house to collect the next rental payment in a month to see how they were maintaining the house. I was so disappointed when I visited and saw the damage. The man was an alcoholic who had smashed the kitchen cabinets with a hammer and used the floors as a bathroom. I gave them 30 days to vacate the house.

This experience turned my heart towards prejudice against this nationality of people. When I started attending the prayer meetings, I would sit in the back row, and the Lord was touching me in many ways during these meetings. At one meeting, I prayed, asking the Lord to help me get rid of this prejudice. Just after that, about eight people from the same nationality that had rented the house sat around me. Then Peter who had the spiritual gift of prophecy took the microphone and said some of us had felt prejudice towards others. He asked us to turn to the people around us and ask for forgiveness. I turned to those around me, asked for forgiveness, and we hugged each other. The prejudice left me in an instant. I marveled at the lengths God would go to heal a heart not in sync with His.

There was another time, while attending a church conference, we found ourselves sitting in a pew next to someone with whom I had had disagreements over time. Forgiving this person had been a challenge for me. I knew that Jesus forgives me and wants me to forgive others. After the event, I took my glasses out of the pocket in the pew and went home. When I got home, I realized the glasses I had taken were not mine. I called the person beside whom I had been sitting, and they confirmed they had my glasses and invited me over to exchange them.

When we arrived, the person welcomed us in, offered us a little treat, and we had a good talk. During that conversation, the Lord washed away the unforgiveness from my heart. It was clear that the Lord had orchestrated that situation to help me let go of the unforgiveness I had been holding onto.

A Divine Message in the Crowd

Before my Renewal experience and relationship with the Lord, I was hesitant to teach catechism, fearing that a child's question might stump me. However, with my newfound faith, I felt bold and volunteered to teach young children in our parish. I received many insights from the Holy Spirit on how to present the teachings. One child, whose parents never attended Mass, was dropped off each week. The child was so enthusiastic about what he learned that he encouraged his parents to join him at weekly Mass. Twenty years later, they were still faithfully attending.

This was a fulfillment of a vision at a church event featuring Fr. Stenzel and Rev. Stanley. When we were invited to attend, initially I hesitated, but at the last minute, I felt that God had a message for me if I went. I told Natalie and our son Wayne that I needed to attend because God had something to tell me. I decided to wear a suit and tie.

The church was packed, and we found seats in the middle of the crowd. During the event, one of the speakers pointed at me and said, "You in the suit stand up, I have a message for you from the Lord." He then shared a vision of me writing on a chalkboard. I was teaching.

Choosing Love Over Meetings

At one point, my work for the Renewal required me to travel twice a year for 5-day meetings. I really didn't like being away from Natalie for so long. I missed Natalie so much. We were both so happy when I came home. I remember coming down the escalator at the airport and seeing Natalie with a big smile greeting me. Eventually, I gave up attending those meetings and appointed someone else to go in my place.

Natalie and I have always worked together. When I

had a real estate company, she kept all the listings up to date for me. When I changed the taps in our home, she was right there assisting me. While I was building homes, she handled all our banking and bookkeeping. If I needed lumber, she would take our truck and pick it up. One time, she accidentally stepped on the accelerator too hard and dropped a load of oak finishing material on the road. Some cars behind her ran over the material, leaving tire tracks on our beautiful oak panels.

A Remodeling Mishap: The Broken Nose Incident

In December 2019, our niece bought her first home. The stairway to the basement needed remodeling because anyone going down the stairs would hit their head on a beam. Natalie and I worked on this project together. While I was putting up a frame to hold a handrail, Natalie stood on the opposite side of the stairs. I was tapping a 2x4 to make sure it was level, and it accidentally swung across the stairway and hit Natalie in the nose. Her nose started bleeding profusely. I quickly rushed her to the hospital, where they confirmed her nose was broken. The next day, she had black eyes from the injury.

Later, when we were purchasing travel insurance, the agency asked if either of us had been to the emergency room in the past year. I said, "Yes, Natalie has." They asked, "What was she in for?" I replied, "I broke her nose." They looked shocked, probably thinking I was some kind of abuser, but after explaining the situation, we all had a good laugh about it.

The Flying Mattress: A Winter Mishap

One time, my brother, Msgr. Stan, ordered a new mattress. He asked me if I would pick it up for him. I put the mattress in the back of my pickup truck, but I did not tie it down. It was wintertime and at one point I saw this object flying by in my rear-view mirror and it was his mattress. It shot right across the street and a car going in the opposite direction rode over it, got hung up on it and burned a big hole in it. The next Sunday at Mass in the church where he was a pastor, he told the story of the mattress to the whole congregation. I couldn't help it, I burst out laughing out loud in the church.

The Unexpected Rider: A Motorcycle Tale

One evening after a prayer meeting, a group of us gathered around a young man and his new motorcycle. I asked if I could sit on it, and he agreed. I started asking him about the various controls, like what the lever and foot pedal did. Then, I asked if he could start the engine so I could hear it. As soon as he did, I threw it into gear and sped off. Natalie later told me his jaw dropped because he had no idea, I knew how to ride a motorcycle. She quickly assured him that it's O.K., that

I had a motorcycle. Just another one of my mischievous pranks!

So, You Want to Build Your Own House, Eh?

In 1976, we were inspired to build our own home after visiting some display homes. Despite having no prior building experience, we decided to go for it. The city of Winnipeg had some lots for sale, and the process involved submitting a bid with a deposit of 10% of the price. On the day the bids were opened at City Hall, we were thrilled to find out that our bid, which was just above the reserve price, had secured the lot we wanted.

We bought a book of house plans and found one we liked. After asking an architect to make some revisions, we submitted the plan to the city permit department, and it was approved. With no experience dealing with tradespeople, I visited several construction sites to gather names and contacts.

A city official came to mark the level of the finished grade for our home. I hired Steve, a basement contractor, who staked out the property and began construction. It was exciting to watch as Steve used his huge caterpillar to excavate the basement area, marking the depth according to the city's guidelines. He installed the piling, formed the basement walls, and placed the reinforced steel and floor joists. One morning, as he was ready to pour the basement concrete, I realized the house seemed too high out of the ground. The finished grade looked halfway up the trees.

I rushed to the city permit department, explaining that the concrete was about to be poured, and the house appeared too high out of the ground. I threatened legal action if there was a mistake in marking the final grade. Within 20 minutes, four city officials arrived on-site. They pointed out to me that the mark indicated we should cut two feet deeper for the final grade. Unfortunately, the contractor had missed this detail, and we were two feet too high.

Frustrated, the contractor dismantled everything, threw the materials into the excavated hole, and left, saying, "I'm out of here." I was stressed and unsure of what to do next. Three days later, Steve returned, reset everything, jackhammered the piles and dug down two feet, and finally poured the basement concrete.

Steve's crew had a habit of cursing frequently, which made me very uncomfortable. I mentioned this to Steve, and the next time someone on his crew swore, Steve corrected them, saying, "Don't say that. Say 'Gee Whizz' instead." After that, I didn't hear any more swearing from the crew.

We needed a carpenter to frame the building, and my lawyer recommended someone for the job. I took my plans to this person, and after a week, he quoted me a price. I agreed, and he started the job.

On his first day, he nailed down the subfloor. When I came to check on the progress, I found him sitting on the plywood, staring at the plans. I asked what the problem was, and he admitted he didn't know how to build an alcove for a china cabinet in the dining room. I was frustrated and asked why he took the job if he didn't know how to build it, especially after having the plans for a week. He reacted aggressively, coming at me with a hammer and saying, "They should have killed all you people off in the last war."

I immediately called my lawyer, who had referred

him. My lawyer told me to come to his office the next morning to settle the issue. At the meeting, the framer demanded $2000 for the work he had done in one day. My lawyer advised me to pay him to avoid a lien on my property. Reluctantly, I wrote a check for $2000 and returned to the site.

That day the city building inspector visited and asked about the framer. I explained the situation, and he said I should never have paid $2000 for such minimal work. The original contract was for $3000. I quickly contacted my bank to stop the payment, but the framer had already cashed the check. Later, I discovered that my lawyer was also representing the framer. That lawyer was eventually incarcerated for defrauding a Catholic church out of a large sum of money.

I found two young men who were framing carpenters, and they agreed to work on weekends since they had full-time jobs. I gave them the go-ahead, but after doing a little bit of work, they decided it was summertime and they wanted to go to the beach instead, so they quit.

Next, I found another man who said he could do the job. At this point, we were framing the roof rafters.

One of the rafters he put up was badly bowed. When I asked him why he installed such a crooked piece, he said he would fix it. He cut the rafter in half, nailed a 2x4 to it, and declared it good. I decided to let him go.

Finding someone to finish the framing job became difficult. Most said they couldn't give me a fixed price since the job had already been started; they could only offer an hourly rate. Eventually, someone referred me to a group of five men who traveled together in a bus and worked as a team to frame buildings. I agreed to hire them.

However, I soon noticed that while two men were framing, the other three stood around with their arms folded, watching. I was paying five men by the hour, but only two were working. After many stressful days, this part of the building was finally completed, but I ended up paying much more than I should have.

When you took out a building permit back then, there was a publication listing all the homes being built and who took out the permits. A plumber saw this publication and called me, offering to give me a quote for the job. He provided a quote on a small piece of paper, which I accepted, and I authorized him to start the work.

I expected him to begin immediately, but three days passed with no sign of him. When I called to inquire, he bluntly said he wouldn't do the job for the quoted amount. I reminded him that he had given me a written quote, to which he responded, "You know what you can do with that paper." With no other plumber available and the project ready to proceed, I reluctantly paid him the extra money.

The plumber's delay reminded me of a story I once heard. In a communist country, a man wanted to buy a car. He was told he had to pay the full price upfront and then come back in 10 years to pick it up. The man asked, "Should I come in the morning or the afternoon?" The salesperson, puzzled, replied, "It's 10 years from now. Why does it matter?" The man answered, "Because the plumber is coming in the morning."

I submitted my plan to a heating company for a quote and gave them the go-ahead to do the job. The installer was running the heating pipes to the second floor, but instead of placing them along the wall and between the ceiling joists, he had them exposed and protruding into the room. I asked him why he was installing the pipes this way. He replied, "Oh, you can just box around the pipes." I insisted that he redo them correctly. He said it would cost extra. I made sure he straightened out the pipes, and he eventually finished the rest of the job properly.

I decided to save some money by painting the house myself. The roof was quite steep with a 9/12 pitch, and there were two dormers that needed painting. To prevent myself from falling off the roof, I thought I needed some extra support. I got our son, Rick, to sit on one side of the dormer. I tied a rope to him, flipped it over the dormer, and tied the other end around myself. In hindsight, this was not a good idea, and I thank God that neither of us slipped off the roof.

We had many more negative experiences during this construction. I often joked that I should write a book entitled "So You Want to Build Your Own House, Eh?"

Faith in the Face of Adversity: Our Construction Journey

After living in this new house for a few months, we decided to move to Southern California. We applied for and received green cards for all six of us. We made three trips there but ultimately decided not to move.

Having sold our house, we began building a new one. A man named Morris frequently visited, asking to buy the house. We told him it was for ourselves. We had ordered reclaimed brick, which was trendy at the time, but once it was installed, we hated it. I called Morris and offered to sell him the house, and he accepted.

Later, another man approached Morris, inquiring about the builder of his house. That man contacted us, marking the beginning of our building business.

We took several risks by building houses on spec, meaning we didn't have buyers lined up and hoped to sell them quickly. In 1979, we approached our credit union manager for a $250,000 loan to build a house for sale, which was a significant amount at the time. He immediately approved the loan. We built a house for ourselves and another one for sale. However, interest rates began to rise sharply, and we found ourselves paying 20% interest on the borrowed money. The construction business slowed down, so I started painting houses, and Natalie took a job in an isolated office on the tenth floor of a building in a rough part of town. Despite our efforts, our combined income couldn't cover the interest payments.

During this period, the evening news frequently reported on the severe recession, highlighting how real estate wasn't moving and many builders were going bankrupt. They even showed our house with a for-sale sign on the news, which was disheartening. This struggle continued for a year. One night, feeling utterly desperate, I woke up at 3:00 a.m. and cried out to Jesus for help. In 1 Cor. 10:13, it says God is faithful and he will not let you be tested beyond your strength. Praying intensely, I said, "I know that you will not let us be tried beyond our strength, but Lord, I am at the end of my strength."

The next day, we received a letter from a person who identified as a born-again Christian. He had seen our house for sale six months earlier and offered to buy it for nearly our asking price in cash. Overjoyed, I said,

"Natalie, you're not going to believe it, but our house is sold!" Our prayers had been answered.

NATALIE

Singing Through the Storm: A Story of Faith

When the house we built didn't sell for a year, it caused many sleepless nights and a lot of anxiety. I love to read, and sometimes I would buy books and put them on the shelf to read later. One day, I felt led to pick up a book by Merlin Carrothers called "Power in Praise." In it, Carrothers shared that he always praised God, no matter the situation, good or bad, and the Lord was always there to help him. So, I put the book down and thought, "O.K. Lord, I'm going to start singing and praising you right now, even though I don't feel like it. And someday when we come out of our trial, I'll witness about your power."

I kept this to myself, not even telling Richard. After a week of praising, the heavy feeling lifted, and I felt a deep inner joy. It bubbled over one evening at the dinner table. Our sons looked at me as if I had flipped and asked how come I was so happy. I told them about praising the Lord.

Two weeks later, at a prayer group leadership meeting, a woman mentioned that someone from Dauphin, Manitoba, wanted speakers from Winnipeg for a Renewal Weekend. She then turned to Richard and me and said, "I really feel that the Lord wants you to go and speak on Praise and Thanksgiving."

My heart skipped a beat. No one knew about my conversation with God about witnessing. I knew we had to go. I knew God was asking us to go.

At first, I wondered why God wanted us to share before our financial trial ended. After the weekend, I understood that God wanted to show people that His joy could be present even in the middle of a trial because I shared about our trial and what happened when I praised the Lord. They could see that my joy was genuine and not faked.

RICHARD

From Bids to Blessings: A Story of Divine Partnership

There came a time when I was offering excellent

prices for building homes but couldn't close any deals. One day, Natalie brought home a book titled "Good Morning, Lord" from a local bookstore. It told the story of a Christian man whose business had faltered. He decided to make the Lord his partner, pledging to give 10% of his earnings to charity. His business thrived so much that he had to hire someone to manage the charitable donations. At that time, we were donating about 4% of our income to charities. Inspired by the book, I decided to follow the same plan and commit 10% of our earnings to charity.

We had previously tried to purchase a vacant lot to build on, but each time I bid, someone else won. When the city put up six lots for sale, I bid on all six, hoping to get at least one. I had to put up 10% of the bid price for each property. On the day the bids were opened at City Hall, I ended up winning all six lots. I was shocked because I didn't have the money to pay for them. On the way home, I was so distracted that I even drove through a red light. Once home, Natalie and I opened our Bible and prayed fervently. The passage we read was, *"They shall build houses."* (Isaiah 65:21)

Within an hour, we received a phone call from someone who had also bid on the lots. He offered us $5,000 more than we had paid for one of the lots. We gladly accepted, relieved to have one less property to pay for. Over the next year, I earned a quarter of a million dollars from building on those lots, which was a significant amount at the time.

Committing to making the Lord our business partner led to a substantial increase in profits. We were able to give away more money the following year than we had earned the year before. Over the years, we have honored our commitment to the Lord and have never looked back. He has always provided for us abundantly.

Faith on the Job: Sharing and Impacting Lives

While we were building houses, I often shared my faith with the workers, leading to some great discussions. About 20 years later, while camping at Birds Hill Park, a man approached us and said he remembered me from when he installed carpet in one of our homes. I was surprised and asked how he could remember me from just that one job. He explained that his father, a member of the Christian Reformed Church, had always told his children that the Catholic faith was not true and was a cult. However, during our conversation while he was installing the carpet, he realized that the Jesus I believed in as a Catholic was the same Jesus he believed in. This revelation dispelled all the negative things his father had said about the Catholic faith. Imagine, 20 years later!

When we step out in faith and share with others, we never know the true impact. As the Scriptures say, we plant the seed, and God will water it.

Sometimes we would have a customer over for dinner, someone for whom we were building a house. This didn't stop us from praying after dinner and we never sensed any unease from our customers.

Power of a Prayer Card: A Faith Story

I remember a time when a lady from Vancouver called and asked if we could visit her brother, who was dying in the hospital. My first thought was that he should be anointed by a priest. When I mentioned this to her, she said he had already been anointed but still didn't believe in Jesus. I went to the hospital to visit him, made some small talk to break the ice, and then asked if I could pray for him. He declined, saying his family was praying for him and that was enough. I asked if I could leave my business card, which had a prayer of surrendering one's life to the Lord on the reverse side. He agreed, so I left it on the table.

Feeling disappointed, I called his sister in Vancouver and told her what had happened. She suggested that he might listen to a nurse. I knew a nurse from our prayer meeting who worked at that hospital, so I asked her to visit him. About a week later, the nurse called me and said, "Do you know what he was doing when I went to see him? He was reciting the prayer that you left for him." Once again, it shows that we plant the seed, and God will water it.

Healing in His Time: Mrs. Golub's Miracle

Shortly after we were prayed over for an outpouring of the Holy Spirit, both Natalie and I felt inspired to serve the Lord in any way we could. I volunteered to take Holy Communion to the sick in our parish every Friday. Our priest asked me to visit a 92-year-old lady named Mrs. Golub, suggesting that she would be delighted if I greeted her in Polish. When I greeted her in Polish, she was overjoyed. I decided not only to bring her Holy Communion but also to pray for her. I asked if there was anything specific, she wanted prayer for, and she mentioned that she couldn't hear in one of her ears. I immediately felt certain that God would heal her.

Recalling how Jesus healed in the Bible, I prayed for her and blew into her ear. I then asked her if she could hear, but she said, "No, it is the same." I was so sure she would be healed. The following Friday, I eagerly asked about her hearing, but it was still the same. We prayed again, and I repeated the process, but there was no change.

On the third Friday, as soon as I walked in, she exclaimed that she could hear perfectly. She explained that after I left the previous week, she had taken a nap, and when she woke up, something fell out of her ear. It was the lead from a .22-caliber bullet. She recounted that as a child in Europe, someone had been cleaning a gun and accidentally fired it, hitting her in the cheek. Her ear bled for several days. Although she could hear initially, she lost hearing in that ear about 30 years ago. God had healed her, not in my time, but in His time, which in this case was a couple of weeks. This was a witness of God's goodness and his healing power to the parishioners because the priest spoke about it at Mass.

The Healing Power of Prayer: A Caregiver's Miracle

When it was my turn to distribute Holy Communion at Mass, I would always ask the Holy Spirit to shine through me so that I would reflect Jesus to the people coming forward. The same was true when Natalie and I brought Holy Communion to people in their homes when they were sick. We would ask if they had any prayer intentions and pray for them. We wanted them to experience the presence of the Lord through the Eucharist and personal prayer.

Kathleen, a woman with ALS, was one who would ask for prayer after receiving Holy Communion because she always felt peace. We had to be very careful when we visited her because she had almost no immunity. When we entered her home, we had to wash and sanitize our hands and take other precautions. She required a caregiver 24/7. One day, when we arrived, her caregiver was quite sick, coughing and sneezing. We wondered why she was there, given the patient's need for protection. We asked the caregiver if we could pray for her, and she agreed.

The next time we brought Holy Communion, Kathleen said, "Your prayers are very powerful. Do you remember when you prayed for my caregiver who was sick? After you left, she lay down for 10 minutes, got up, and was completely healthy." God didn't want a sick person looking after Kathleen and we were so happy that God had used us to heal this person.

Faithful Leadership: Called to Serve

One morning, I woke up with a strong feeling that the Lord was saying we would lead the prayer group we had been attending. I asked Natalie if the Lord had spoken to her the previous night. She confirmed, saying the Lord had told her the same thing.

After a year of attending the prayer meetings, the leader, Deacon Nick, asked if we could take over while he went on a three-week holiday. We agreed. When he returned, I told him he could resume his role, but he suggested we continue for a bit longer. That "bit longer" turned into 12 years.

There was a Jesuit priest at St. Paul's College at the University of Manitoba who was a dear friend to exchange students from China. His name was Fr. Braceland. One of the exchange students, named Peter, attended our prayer meeting and later returned to China, where he started 14 prayer groups in Hong Kong.

When Fr. Braceland passed away, these students attended his funeral, each placing a red rose on his coffin. It was beautiful to see how much they loved and respected him.

We witnessed many inspiring stories among the group members. One lady, named Anne, had recently lost her husband and was feeling very sad. In her prayer, she told God that she had no one to dig up her garden. Miraculously, a man appeared at her door and asked if there was anything he could do for her. She asked if he could dig up the garden, and he agreed. She intended to pay him, but when she looked out the window to check on his progress, she saw that the garden had been completely dug up, and the man was gone.

Anne's story reminded me of another one I had read. There was an old gentleman who lived alone in New Jersey. He wanted to plant his annual tomato garden but was unable to do so because the ground was too hard. His son, Vincent, who used to help him, was in prison and couldn't assist. The old man wrote a letter to his son describing his predicament:

"Dear Vincent, I am feeling sad because I won't be able to plant my tomato garden this year. I'm just getting too old to dig up the garden plot. I know if you were here, my troubles would be over. I know you would be happy to dig the plot for me, like in the old days. Love, Papa."

A few days later, he received a letter from his son:

"Dear Papa, don't dig up that garden, that's where the bodies are buried. Love, Vinny."

At 4:00 a.m. the next morning, the FBI and local police arrived at the old man's home, digging up the entire garden plot but finding no bodies. They apologized to the old man and left. The next day, the old man received another letter from his son:

"Dear Pop, go ahead and plant those tomatoes now. That's the best I could do under the circumstances. Love, Vinny."

NATALIE

Faith: Trusting God's Promise

Just as God walked with Adam and Eve in the Garden, He desires to walk and talk with us today.

In 2014, I had a persistent cough. On June 24th, my doctor informed me that something showed up on my left lung, possibly cancer. I was devastated. When we got home, I went to my prayer corner and asked the Lord for a message. I randomly opened the Bible to Haggai 2:18-19: *"Consider from this day forward: from the twenty-fourth day of the ninth month..... From this day, I will bless!"*

I took this as a sign that the Lord was looking after me, especially since the day in the Scripture matched my appointment day. I clung to that message, quoting it every time I prayed about my concern.

A few days later, I noticed a correction in my Bible's notes. It clarified that the passage actually referred to the twenty-fourth day of the sixth month, which was the exact date of my doctor's appointment. This reinforced my belief that the Lord would bless me.

Thankfully, further tests showed that I did not have cancer. The Lord hears the cry of the poor.

From Enforcement to Empathy: An Officer's Journey

At a large prayer group meeting at St. John Brebeuf Church, Leonard, a drug enforcement officer, shared how God was working in his life. As an RCMP officer, he questioned whether a Christian could do his job and considered changing his occupation.

God gave him a Scripture passage about delivering him from his enemies, and God impressed upon his heart that the people trafficking in cocaine were not his enemies. The true enemies were the drugs, the principalities and powers, the rulers of this world of darkness, and the evil spirits in regions above.

Leonard began praying for the people involved. He laughed, saying, "Who'd have thought a few years ago, I'd be praying for the Hell's Angels." He also felt led to pray, "Lord, deliver the enemy, the drugs, into Your hands." A week later, he was involved in a huge drug bust.

Leonard noticed his attitude changing towards the people involved. In this case, it was two very young women, pawns in the hands of their bosses. One was even thankful she was caught because of her severe cocaine habit.

He felt deep compassion for them and saw the Lord working in their hearts through their conversations. He also noticed a change in his fellow officers. After speaking with the head of his department, he believed the young women would be sent to rehabilitation rather than prosecuted.

God is truly a God of second chances.

When Words Fail: The Power of Silent Intercession

Sometimes, during a Life in the Spirit Seminar, we would have participants sit in a circle, and then each team member would go behind them and pray for every individual, one at a time, moving around the circle.

I always felt inadequate during these times because I didn't have prophetic words for people like the others on the team. I felt I had nothing to offer since I couldn't provide a word from the Lord that was just for them. What I did was pray for more of the Holy Spirit in their lives and for more of God's love to be poured out on them.

During a seminar in Virden, I shared my feelings with the Lord in my heart. After the prayer session, one lady shared that everyone had a word for her except one person. She said that when that person stood behind her, she felt as if an angel was there, and she felt the love of the Lord.

The Lord is quick to answer! He is so good! He wants to encourage and affirm us.

Windows to the Divine: Experiencing God's Love and
Presence

I never knew what it was like to sit on a daddy's lap or receive good fatherly advice. However, through the grace of experiencing God's love for me since we have been in the Charismatic Renewal, and his gift of four sons and my soulmate, Richard, I can say that void has been filled.

When people are receiving prayer, they usually close their eyes. Once, when Fr. McAleer was in Winnipeg and people went up for prayer, he asked them to open their eyes and look into his eyes. When it was my turn, I looked into his eyes and saw the colored part light up, becoming brighter and brighter, then moving around. It was a very bright, pulsating light radiating such love and joy. I knew it was God, and I felt He was telling me He was so pleased with me.

I was stunned but said nothing, thinking everyone experienced this. The next morning, I found out from Richard that it wasn't the case. When I asked Fr. McAleer about it, he said he didn't know it had happened, though someone else had mentioned a similar experience once. For me, it was another healing moment in my journey of experiencing the love of God.

We were in Edmonton, Alberta for an event when a lady approached me and said, "You don't remember me, but I was at an event in Winnipeg a few months ago, and I saw Jesus looking at me through your eyes. His eyes are brown, but your eyes are blue."

I thought back and vaguely remembered being at a registration table or something similar. I recalled her because she had a quizzical look on her face as she walked away. I also remembered helping her with something and feeling a sense of kindness toward her.

Reinhard Bonnke shared an experience he had in Africa. He went to a music store to purchase a piano for his ministry. The store clerk turned pale and said, "I see Jesus in your eyes." After leaving the store, Reinhard asked Jesus in his heart, "How is it that he saw You in my eyes?" The response he received was, "I do live in you, and sometimes I like to look out the windows."

Miracles and Ministry: A Testament to God's Faithfulness

God's voice is a very gentle and loving voice. One

night, I woke up and heard Him say, "You shall work for me." And my thought was, "Full time?" Though I didn't hear an audible answer, I knew in my heart it was full time. I told Richard the next morning what happened, but we kept it to ourselves, believing that if it was from the Lord, it would happen.

In 1988, several years later, we were asked to work full time for the Catholic Charismatic Renewal Services of Manitoba. What a privilege it has been! God gave us the boldness to step out in faith and invite his crème-de-la-crème speakers in the Renewal, and He didn't disappoint us. Our list of speakers reads like a who's who of the Charismatic Renewal. People often asked, "How do you get all the big names in the Renewal to come to Winnipeg?"

When Sr. Briege McKenna, who has a worldwide healing ministry, came to Winnipeg, the event was held at the Concert Hall, which has a capacity of 2,200. We sold out. People phoned, asking if they could stand in the aisles. Of course we couldn't allow that due to fire regulations. I had to laugh when one lady even said she'd sit on someone's lap! During the weekend, people were in the lobby asking if anyone had a spare ticket.

When Fr. McDonough was giving a talk at the University of Manitoba, I was sitting in the back row next to a woman who kept asking her friend, "What did he say?" Fr. McDonough spoke quietly and gently, so it didn't seem like anything extraordinary was happening. At the end of his talk, he simply asked, "The Lord has been healing people. How many of you can now hear?"

The woman beside me suddenly asked her friend, "Why is he shouting?" I thought he's not shouting, and then I realized she had been healed and could now hear!

Another time, Richard and I were involved in a Life in the Spirit seminar at a minimum security prison at Milner Ridge. While praying for one of the prisoners for the release of the Holy Spirit, the man started sobbing deeply. We wondered what God was doing in his heart. Finally, when he was able to speak, we were deeply touched when we heard him say, "I now have an identity."

Many deacons and priests have emerged from the Renewal, including our own son. God inspired one young man to go to Radway and then return to start a Bible School in St. Malo.

Using a video on Charisms from the U.S. National Service Committee, we conducted workshops in country prayer groups. We encouraged people who had never prayed for anyone to pray for the sick. In a remote northern village, one woman was overcome with laughter, falling to her knees. This was God's joy being poured into her. When she stood up, her long-standing hip problem was gone, and she could walk.

In another town, there was friction between two prayer group leaders. One had a hearing problem. We had the other leader pray for him. God reconciled them, and the hearing problem was healed.

When the Fraternity of Priests group began in Manitoba, a 77-year-old priest traveled three hours each way once a week to attend their meetings. He wouldn't miss it, saying, "What a wonderful way to prepare for death."

A Life in the Spirit Seminar was held for a Confirmation class in a small town. The Sister said she had never seen youth so ready for Confirmation. Some of the youth said they came because their parents told them to, but they stayed because they wanted to.

The most amazing Life in the Spirit Seminar we saw was in Rome at the Sant' Ignazio Church. Fr. Faricy told us he was going to conduct the baptism in the Holy Spirit session. When he mentioned, "It's going to be crowded, 5,000 people," we said, "What? We're going to go and see this." When we arrived, we could barely get through the door. It was shoulder to shoulder with people. Fr. Faricy was at the front of the church by the altar. He told us to put our hands on the person next to us as he led the prayer. What an awesome sight!

That trip was very special because we had the opportunity to meet Pope St. John Paul II in the Papal Audience Hall. On Wednesday mornings, around 10,000 people fill that hall to see and hear the Pope. 100 are permitted to go up and personally meet the Pope. Fr. Rick applied for the three of us and we were overjoyed to see the ticket slipped under our door the evening before. We were escorted to the front row and at the end of the Pope's message, each group went up the stairs to where he was sitting. It's a brief but precious moment with the Pope, and the photographer captured it all. We bought every photo. Fr. Rick introduced us and mentioned our work with the Charismatic Renewal, and Pope St. John Paul II blessed our ministry!

Hearts can be touched, and lives changed by the power of the Holy Spirit. I was once asked to read a Scripture passage at a funeral. I really wanted that Scripture passage to be meaningful to the people there. So, I asked the Lord to anoint the words as I read them.

After the funeral, I received a thank-you card from the daughter, who wrote, "Your reading of the Scripture at mom's funeral Mass made its meaning more clear to me. Thank you." That's what the Holy Spirit can do through any one of us. All we need to do is ask.

Heaven-Sent: The Mysterious Woman Who Saved Lauren

On October 1, 2015, our granddaughter Lauren was attending Umpqua Community College in Roseburg, Oregon. She also worked in the library to help with college expenses, so she was often on campus.

That day, she left the library and was about to go through another building to reach her car in the parking lot. A woman stopped her from going in, warning her that there was a shooter inside that building. She told Lauren to go to another building and stay there. The shooter, a 26-year-old student, fatally shot an assistant professor and nine students, injuring nine others.

This woman saved Lauren's life. Lauren never saw her before or after that day. Was it an angel? Whether it was an angelic being or a human, God sent her! We believe this was an answer to our prayers, as we pray daily for our children, grandchildren, and great-grandchildren.

God's Wink

Sometimes, God gives us a little wink. Richard was scheduled for radiation on an enlarged cancerous lymph node in his neck at 1:35 p.m. on September 19, 2024. However, he was taken in just after 1:00 p.m. because someone was late for their appointment. When we got home, there was a message from our sister-in-law, Anna. She knew Richard was going to get treatment but didn't remember the date. Yet, at 1:00 p.m., she felt compelled to pray for Richard. Many people were praying for him, but this felt like a special reminder that God cared and was with Richard through this journey. After this treatment, the lump was gone.

One Sunday morning, Richard woke up not feeling well at all. So much so, he didn't go to church with me. Before Mass, I was in deep prayer asking the Lord to heal Richard. Suddenly, I felt a break in my spirit. I felt that the Lord answered my prayer, and I could hardly wait to get home to find out. Richard was in the kitchen fully healed, preparing our lunch. When I asked when he started feeling better, he said it was just before Mass would have started.

RICHARD

Miracles of Support: God's Hand in Our Ministry

After leading the prayer group, we were asked to be on the board of directors of the Service Committee for the Catholic Charismatic Renewal Services of Manitoba (CCRS). Then in 1988, when the service committee approached us, asking if we would work for them full time, they explained that they didn't have much money but could offer us a starting salary of $12,000 a year each, with future salaries depending on donations. The Lord had already prepared us for this both spiritually and financially. We gladly accepted, knowing in our hearts that this was our calling from the Lord.

At one point, donations were becoming scarce, and we wondered if this was a sign from the Lord that perhaps He didn't want this work to continue. After praying about this, I received a phone call from a man who used to attend our events. He asked if he could come over that morning.

When he arrived, he handed me a cheque made out to the Renewal for $10,000, saying he hoped it would be of help. This experience showed me that you can never outdo the Lord. Another time, when we were short of money, we gave a seminar in Boissevain, Manitoba. After the seminar, a gentleman wrote to us, saying he really liked what we were doing and enclosed a cheque for $10,000 for our work. It's so encouraging to receive these confirmations from the Lord for what you are doing in His ministry.

We initially worked eight years for CCRS while still managing our real estate and building business. Then, we transitioned to full-time service, bringing our total tenure to 35 years. We retired at the age of 80. In our final year of service, we conducted 14 Life in the Spirit Seminars across 14 parishes, held several live conferences, and operated an office for the Renewal.

We feel incredibly privileged to have been part of this work of God. It has been a profoundly blessed experience that we wouldn't trade for anything. So much so, that currently we are live streaming a prayer meeting every Wednesday evening. We have attendees from across Canada. When you work for the Lord, there is no retirement.

Counting Blessings: Recognizing God's Gifts in Everyday Life

Sometimes, when you're doing the Lord's work, you can encounter obstacles placed in your path by the devil. I remember one conference we were holding at the University of Manitoba. Just an hour before it began, a huge truck backed into the only entranceway to the conference and dumped a load of asphalt. We quickly called the authorities, and they brought some 4x8 sheets of plywood to cover the fresh asphalt so people could enter the arena.

You could say that sometimes God works in mysterious ways. I remember a couple, Maurice and Barbara, who had a lucrative business in recycling oil. Their property became polluted with PCBs, and the government shut them down, causing them to lose everything, even their car. They said if this hadn't happened, they might never have turned to the Lord.

Just when they had lost everything, they attended their first Catholic conference. They sat in the front row of the Concert Hall. Dana, an Irish singer, was performing a song and, looking right at them, sang, "I have nothing in my pocket, and I don't feel bad." God truly has a sense of humor.

Barbara later passed away, and Maurice became a priest, ministering in the Peace River country.

This reminds me of a story about counting our blessings. Even if I hadn't been reminded, I still wanted to share it.

Two old friends bumped into each other on the street one day. One of them looked forlorn, almost on the verge of tears. His friend asked, "What has the world done to you, my old friend?"

The sad fellow replied, "Three weeks ago, an uncle died and left me $40,000." "That's a lot of money," his friend said.

"But you see," the sad fellow continued, "two weeks ago, a cousin I never even knew died and left me $85,000." "Sounds like you've been blessed, my friend."

"You don't understand," he interrupted. "Last week, my great aunt passed away, and I inherited almost a quarter of a million dollars." Now the friend was really confused. "Then why do you look so glum?" "This week, nothing."

If we stopped and thought about it, we would recognize the many blessings we have in life.

A man who owned a small estate wanted to sell it. He called a real estate agent and asked him to write an advertisement describing the house and land. When the ad was ready, the agent read it to the owner. "Read that again," said the owner. The agent read the description once more. "I don't think I will sell after all," said the owner. "I've been looking for an estate like that all my life, and I didn't know that I owned it."

Helen Keller once said, "When one door of happiness closes, another opens; but often we look so long at the closed door that we do not see the one which has been opened for us."

God's Hand in My Life

When I was around 20, I drove right through a stop sign at Salter Street and was hit broadside by a car. The impact pushed in my driver's door and the whole left side of my car. I ended up with a lump the size of a goose egg on my head, but through it all, God had a plan for me and looked after me.

Several years ago, I had another freak accident. We were in Washington state, and I slipped on a service station bathroom floor, falling backward and hitting my head on the concrete. The sound of my head hitting the floor was like dropping a pumpkin. I was dazed and shaking, and I barely managed to walk to the car to tell Natalie what had happened. But God had a plan, and I was O.K.

At the age of 73, I found myself completely out of breath even after walking just a few feet. I couldn't walk from my car to the grocery store without feeling utterly exhausted. One night, I woke up soaking wet with my heart racing and felt very sick. At the hospital, I was diagnosed with atrial fibrillation and put on medication. I was quite concerned, but the doctor assured me that within a week, I would be able to do everything I could do before. God had a plan and looked after me once again.

Recently, I had a medical procedure and was asked if I was claustrophobic. On the morning of the procedure, I prayed for peace and received the word from Philippians 4:13: *"I can do all things through Christ who strengthens me."* During the 20-minute procedure, I kept repeating that Scripture and felt completely at peace. This was another instance where God's goodness was evident in my life. Friends who had prayed over me the week before said the word for me was "Peace".

Frozen Journeys and Unexpected Blessings
We were invited to speak at a prayer group meeting

in Somerset, Manitoba, about 100 miles away. On the day we were set to leave, the temperature had plummeted to minus 40 degrees. We had both a car and a truck, and given the extreme cold, we decided the truck would be the better option.

As we drove down the highway, we suddenly heard a loud bang. We checked but couldn't determine the cause. Upon arriving in Somerset, we stopped at a grocery store to pick up some chocolate bars for the family we were staying with, as they had young children who would appreciate the treat. When we came out of the store, I tried to start the truck and put it into gear, but it wouldn't move. Fortunately, there was a garage repair shop nearby. The mechanic checked the truck and informed us that the transmission fluid had frozen, causing the transmission to burn out. We left the truck there and called the prayer group leaders, who picked us up and took us to the church.

The leaders lived on a farm several miles from town. After the prayer meeting, we were riding back to their home when the dash lights in their car lit up, steam poured from under the hood, and the car stalled on a country road. Gerald, the driver, saw a light from a farmhouse in the distance and decided to walk there for help. We advised against it, given the long distance and the minus 40-degree temperature. As we grew colder, we prayed for help. Suddenly, a car came down the road and rescued us, taking us to Gerald's home. The following day, we realized that the farmhouse Gerald had planned to walk to was quite a few miles away.

Our vehicle was towed 100 miles back to Winnipeg, where we had the transmission replaced at a significant cost. The tow truck operator mentioned he had been awake for 36 hours due to the high volume of calls for help. We asked how he managed to stay awake for so long, and he said he always eats sunflower seeds while driving; the action of cracking the seeds open keeps him alert.

Once, while driving to a speaking engagement, I pulled into a café on the highway. Natalie asked why I was stopping, and I admitted I had fallen asleep at the wheel. Since that day, I always eat sunflower seeds when driving, a habit I shared with our family, and many of them do the same.

It's That Jesus Guy

We had so many wonderful times organizing events and speaking at seminars. When organizing events, we would inform people by mailing flyers and using a machine called Phonetree to make automated calls. People got used to hearing my voice. One time, I called someone, and a child answered the phone and shouted to their mother, "It's that Jesus Guy!" I thought it was quite funny.

Mistaken Identities: Funny Moments at the Airport

Over 35 years, we brought in more than 300 speakers. One of the speakers we invited was Fr. Gerald Tingley from the Maritimes. We didn't know what he looked like, as we had not yet met him. Fr. Tingley's staff told us he would be wearing a navy sports jacket and a white turtleneck. So, five of us went to the airport dressed in navy sports jackets and white turtlenecks. We stood by the door where passengers exited, repeatedly asking each other, "Are you Fr. Tingley?" We even said it right in front of him, but he just walked

past us, paying no attention.   Our humorous plan
flopped.

Often, when meeting a speaker at the airport, we
didn't know what they looked like. One time, I was
there to meet Dorothy. Everyone, including the flight
crew, had disembarked, and I wondered if our speaker
had missed the flight. I saw a little elderly lady sitting
in a corner of the airport.   Taking a chance, I
approached her and asked if she was Dorothy. She
replied, "Yes, I am."   I mentioned that the photo she
had sent us didn't look like her. She laughed and said,
"That photo is 20 years old, but I like it."

God's Multiplying Effect: From Two to Hundreds

We might never know the ripple effects of God's
plan. Sue Blum, a speaker from Boca Raton, Florida,
was coming to a Bible school near Edmonton, Alberta,
to teach a week-long course on evangelization.   We
decided to attend the course in Radway, Alberta. When
we arrived, we discovered that we were the only two
people who had registered for the course.

Nevertheless, we took the course and, upon returning

home to Winnipeg, we taught it to over 600 people. We were also invited to speak about the course at a conference in Calgary, Alberta. Someone who attended that workshop in Calgary took the course to British Columbia. We could never have imagined what the Lord would accomplish through us by attending that evangelization event. I think it would be normal for a speaker to be disappointed in the turnout but look at what God can do!

NATALIE

Faith and Fortitude: Overcoming Challenges in God's Work

Once, we were in Thompson, Manitoba conducting a Life in the Spirit Seminar. On Saturday afternoon, we attended Mass. I felt the love of the Lord deeply and sang the hymns from my heart. After Mass, a lady in the row ahead of us turned to me and said she was touched by the way I sang the songs. She asked if I was visiting, so I shared about the Life in the Spirit Seminar and guess what .... she came. You never know how God will work through you.

Did you know that Satan dislikes Life in the Spirit

Seminars?   One time, after returning home from praying with people for the baptism in the Holy Spirit, I woke up in the middle of the night and saw a presence in the bedroom that really scared me. I knew it was evil. I felt the bed beside me to see if Richard was there.

I had read that if you encounter something like this, saying the name of Jesus will make it disappear. As I struggled to call out to Jesus, the Scripture passage, *"Even though I walk through the valley of the shadow of death, I will fear no evil, for you are with me,"* (Psalm 23:4) came to mind.   As I mouthed that Scripture, it was gone. The creature disappeared!

This reminded me of when the devil tempted Jesus in the desert, and Jesus responded with Scripture each time. I believe the devil was trying to instill fear in me to stop me from our ministry.

I woke Richard, told him what happened, and we sprinkled the room with Holy Water, prayed, and went back to sleep.

Another time, after returning from a Life in the Spirit Seminar session at Stony Mountain penitentiary, I was sitting on the chesterfield when a pot light in the ceiling above me shattered into pieces. I was covered with hot glass, but not a scratch.

We have a God who protects us from harm. Our Abba, our Daddy, is always with us.

Another time, Richard and I were scheduled to give our testimony at a breakfast in Brandon, Manitoba. There was a bad snowstorm with heavy, wet snow, making driving difficult. On our way to the event, our windshield wipers suddenly stopped working, making it nearly impossible to see. Richard had to open his side window to navigate.

After we gave our testimony and started driving again, the wipers worked perfectly. There had been no problem with them before or after that morning. It was a bit bizarre, but you can guess where that interference was coming from.

The Lord wants to set His people free. We witnessed this when 25 inmates in Stony Mountain maximum security prison participated in the Life in the Spirit Seminar. After the seminar, history was made when these men took part in the first March for Jesus in a Canadian prison, making the headlines.

Later, we learned that a few months before the seminar, God had inspired a group of women from rural Manitoba to walk around the prison, praising God and praying for a mighty outpouring of the Holy Spirit. It gave us goosebumps to realize what God had done. He opened the prison doors to set the prisoners free.

RICHARD

A Rap for Redemption: "Think About It"

Just before the seminar at Stony Mountain, as I was in prayer one morning I felt the Lord was inspiring me to write a rap song. I had never written anything like that before, but I said, "If it's You, Lord, then it will come really easy." It took a couple of minutes. I shared the rap song with the prisoners, and it was a hit with them. It spoke to their hearts.

Think About It

What are you going to do when you start to grow old

When you leave behind all that jewelry and gold

When you plead with the Maker to let you in

But you know that you've committed every kind of sin

Have you thought about your life before today

Where are you heading and what is the way

Well, it's not too late if you do it now

So, turn to the Maker and He will show you how

He will lead you from the darkness into the light

He will take you by the hand to the great delight

He will show you that He loves you through the night and

day

And He will make you happy that you came His way

Won't you think about it now before it's too late

So that someone will be there to open that gate

You've been fooled long enough by the old man's ways

So, do it now and you'll have the length of days

Do it today

The Seminar That Wasn't

We had been invited to give a Life in the Spirit Seminar at Bloodvein Reserve on Lake Winnipeg, scheduled to start on a Friday evening at 7:00 p.m. There were five of us going out for the weekend as speakers. The pastor told us to drive to where the road ended and then take a ferry across the ten-mile lake crossing. This ten-mile channel could get very rough on a windy day.

When we arrived at the ferry, there was no one there to operate it. After waiting for a while, a hydro crew worker came by and asked if we were waiting for the ferry. We said yes, and he informed us that the ferry wouldn't leave until Monday. We then drove over a bridge to an island and asked someone if we could use their phone to call the priest. The priest said he would send a boat to bring us over.

After about an hour, we called the priest again, and he said he couldn't get the boat and would send a plane instead. We waited for over an hour and called him back, only to hear that he couldn't get the plane. He asked us to find a home on the island where someone could put the five of us up for the night, and he would send a boat in the morning.

The person whose phone we were using asked us if we knew what type of boat they would send. It was a 16-foot open type, like a car-top boat, and he warned us that the waves would be 20 feet high the next morning due to strong winds. I imagined us floating somewhere in the middle of the lake in this open boat, with our luggage, and no one ever knowing what happened to us.

I called the priest again and asked how many people had shown up for the seminar. He said one person came, and when we weren't there, they went to play bingo. I told the priest that we would not be coming the next day, and we were heading back home to Winnipeg, and we would send him a video of the seminar that he could show to his people.

From Doubt to Faith: The Prayer Team's Journey

At a large event at St. John Cantius Church with two speakers, the church was packed with attendees. During the time for personal prayer, we were to provide the prayer teams. Over 500 people lined up to receive personal prayer, but we were very short on prayer teams.

I noticed a couple at the back of the church who had just completed a Life in the Spirit Seminar. I asked them to help us pray for the people. They said they didn't know how, so I told them I would show them. We stood together, and people started coming to us. The first person was a lady who said she was blind in one eye. I thought to myself, why couldn't this have been a head cold or something small? I didn't show any outward anxiety and started to pray. After a short while, the lady said, "I can see." I told the couple, "That's how you do it." They continued to pray on their own after that, and many had their prayers answered.

Cardinal Cantalamessa, O.F.M. Cap., Preacher of the Papal Household, stayed with us as he spoke at an event we held.

The Power of Prayer: Fr. McDonough's Healing Services

We read an article about Fr. Edward McDonough, who prayed for a person with two detached retinas, resulting in blindness. The man immediately regained his sight. When he went to see his eye doctor, the doctor said, "You can't see; your retinas are still detached." The man replied, "Well, I can see and am now driving my car."

After reading this article, we decided to invite Fr. McDonough to Winnipeg for a weekend healing conference. One evening, we had him at St. Ignatius Church. His method of prayer was to hold a Holy Hour, during which the Lord would work His healing. Fr. McDonough asked us to have a thermos of coffee in the sacristy, where he went halfway through his presentation to have a smoke and coffee.

He was very low-key in his presentation, and I thought to myself, "Nothing is happening here." At one point, Fr. McDonough asked the packed church, "Can any of you who were not able to hear before, hear now?" About 40 hands went up.

We had another event with him at the University of Manitoba, where we had a huge crowd. People were sitting in rows and rows of metal chairs. Fr. McDonough had a man carrying a gallon of Holy Water, and Fr. would bless each row. All we heard was the clanging of chairs as people slumped to the floor and rested in the Spirit. The Holy Spirit was so powerful at that event; you could just feel the power. It was such a joy to witness this work of God—indeed, such a blessing.

Through Storms and Ice: A Ministry on the Move

One summer, the leadership of our prayer group, which included six people, drove to Steubenville, Ohio, for a prayer group leaders' conference. The conference was held outside in a huge tent with 1,700 leaders present. The praise and worship time was so powerful, with people singing in tongues, that the place was electrified, and many healings began to happen.

Another time, we rented a bus, and 47 of us went to a weekend conference in Langdon, North Dakota. There was a huge snowstorm that weekend, and the roads were blocked, so we couldn't get back to Winnipeg. It was amazing how the people in that parish took all of us into their homes for the night. We were treated royally by the parishioners.

We gladly accepted invitations wherever we were invited. At one point, we even drove over a frozen lake in the winter, hearing the ice crack beneath us. We also drove up north in -50°C weather, on a 250-mile stretch of road with no inhabitants. We saw signs warning, "Do not drive on these roads unless you have winter survival equipment."

One time we were invited to give a seminar in Pine Falls. During the night, there had been freezing rain, and the highways were covered with ice. The trip was 100 miles, but we had made a commitment to be there, so we set out a couple of hours earlier than usual. When we arrived, the people in the parish were very surprised to see us, as they thought we wouldn't come. We felt that if we drove slowly and carefully, we would be safe. It took us twice as long as usual, but we arrived safely.

Kneeling in Awe: The Weeping Statue of Our Lady

When my brother, Msgr. Stan Jaworski, was the pastor of Our Lady of Perpetual Help Church, we had the privilege of using the parish facilities to host numerous seminars. The church almost functioned as a renewal center, often filled with attendees.

On one occasion, we had Fr. Stephen Barham as a speaker. He was an exceptional presenter, delivering inspiring talks and powerful prayers.

One evening, after most of the attendees had left,

about 30 people remained. Fr. Stephen called me to the altar, where there was a statue of the Blessed Virgin Mary. He pointed out that the statue appeared to be crying. When I looked, it was a surreal moment; her face seemed alive. Natalie also saw the face turn to flesh for a moment.

Everyone in the church dropped to their knees, feeling a profound spiritual presence. One person saw that the jewels in the crown on the Blessed Mother were sparkling, while another used a handkerchief to wipe the tears. The experience was brief, but it left an indelible mark on me. I will never forget that evening.

Words of Knowledge: Eileen George's Impactful Visits

We had heard about a speaker named Eileen George from the Boston area, known for her powerful words of knowledge and numerous books. Her events drew huge crowds. We invited her to Winnipeg and a lady who had just lost her husband the previous week attended the event. Eileen, who would customarily walk through the crowd with a microphone, approached this lady and said, "Don't grieve because your husband is with the Lord." This was remarkable because Eileen didn't know this lady, yet her words were profoundly accurate. She shared many other insightful messages with attendees, leaving them deeply blessed. We were so impressed that we invited her back for another successful event.

Eileen had cancer and was very sick, yet she always felt completely healthy while speaking at events, only to feel ill again afterward. I remember going to the Holiday Inn to pick her up for a speaking event. Her entire floor smelled of roses, a phenomenon reported at many of her speaking engagements.

One day, we received a call informing us that Eileen had passed away. Shocked by the news of her death, I called her number to verify. To my surprise, she answered the phone. Unsure of what to say, I invited her to come back for a third time.

A family from the Kenora, Ontario area questioned why we invited her back a third time. They attended the weekend conference, and all were healed. After the conference, they expressed their gratitude, saying they were thrilled we had invited her back for a third time.

FIRE in Winnipeg: Extending Our Tent Pegs

In 1984, we had a conference committee of about eight people. After praying to see whom we should invite for the next annual conference, the names that came to us were Ralph Martin, Fr. John Bertolucci, Fr. Michael Scanlan, and Sr. Ann Shields. Although we never had four speakers at an event before, we decided to write to each of them, inviting them to speak at our conference in Winnipeg. Unfortunately, each one wrote back individually, saying they were unable to come. Our committee was so sure that these were the people God wanted us to invite, but we had to move on.

We then wrote to two other speakers, inviting them for a conference, but they also replied within two weeks, saying they were not able to come. Then, we received a phone call from a gentleman who said he was the organizer of a FIRE rally, where four speakers, the ones we had invited first, had combined their ministries to speak as one group. Their topics for this one-day rally were Faith, Intercession, Repentance, and Evangelization (FIRE). He invited us to attend their first event at the Meadowlands in New Jersey the following weekend to see if it was something we would like to have in Winnipeg.

We gladly accepted the invitation and attended the first FIRE rally with 10,000 people. It was such an inspiring event that we knew we wanted it for Winnipeg. The organizer initially said they couldn't do it that year, maybe the next, but we felt strongly that the Lord was prompting us to invite them for that year.

At lunch, Fr. Scanlan just happened to be sitting opposite us. We encouraged him to bring the team. We also attended a Mass with Fr. Bertolucci and his parents, where we had a chance to speak with him and encourage him to come. The person who drove us around New Jersey was the event organizer, and we tried to persuade him as well.

Eventually, they decided to come at the time we requested. We booked one of the smaller rooms at the Winnipeg Convention Centre. The organizer asked how many people we could expect. We said the last conference had a full house of 1,300 people, so maybe tops 2,000 to 2,500. He said, "How about extending your tent pegs?"

We gulped. The service committee of the Renewal in Manitoba prayed, and someone got the Scripture reading of Jesus feeding the 5,000. We approached the Convention Centre for a larger space, but the room was already booked by a Toronto party. A few days later, they called us back to say the Toronto group had cancelled, and we could have the room that held 5,000.

We ended up having one of the best events ever, with 4,300 people attending. Besides the four speakers, Archbishop Adam Exner gave an excellent homily. We later hosted other FIRE rallies, drawing 3,000 people, and even a satellite rally. Many attendees talked about these rallies for years afterward.

God's Grace in Marriage: Stories of Healing and Hope

A priest invited us to a small community bordering the Northwest Territories to give a Life in the Spirit Seminar and a marriage course for one week in the middle of winter. It took us five separate plane flights to get there. One of the planes was like a tube, and at the entrance, a young lady who looked about 21 years old welcomed us. Before takeoff, she asked if we'd like some juice, which she brought to us. Then, she got into the cockpit as the pilot! At one point, we landed in the middle of a field to pick up a man waiting by his pickup truck.

The priest only had one single bed for the two of us. Natalie slept against the cold winter wall, while I slept on the other side with a chair against the bed to prevent me from falling off. The priest had a dog that had misbehaved, and when scolded, the dog lowered his head and gave a sheepish smile. I had never seen a dog smile like that before.

One of the seminar attendees was the chief of a local Indigenous tribe. He and his wife had been separated for a year. After the marriage seminar, they reconciled, and we heard years later that their marriage was thriving.

Another time, we conducted a marriage course in Portage La Prairie, Manitoba. One couple, who had been having marriage problems, said they had the best summer ever after the course. Sadly, the husband passed away at the end of the summer, but his wife cherished the wonderful memories of their last days together.

We also had a couple attend one of our marriage seminars who were not married but had six children together. When we asked why they hadn't married, the wife said she was afraid because he was an alcoholic. Despite this, they decided to get married after the seminar. From that point on, they said their marriage was terrific. Unfortunately, the husband passed away within a year.

God is so good to have allowed these healings and transformations in these lives.

Different Paths, Same Spirit: The Diverse Ways God Works

We attended a conference with John Wimber at an arena in Detroit, Michigan which drew around 5,000 attendees. The worship sessions were incredible, and after the worship, John Wimber would take the microphone and speak. He would invite the Holy Spirit to come upon us, simply repeating "Come, Holy Spirit" several times and then wait. It was amazing to see people being touched throughout the arena.

Overtime we discovered that God works in different ways through different people. For example, when Fr. Tardif was here for a conference, he would call out healings that took place in the crowd and he would ask the people who were healed to come and testify so everyone could hear. He also wanted confirmation that the words he was receiving were from the Lord. He said he didn't want to say something that was not of the Lord. I recall one person who was in a wheelchair and unable to walk. She was healed, got up, and started to walk around!

On the other hand, Sr. Briege McKenna would call out healings, but she never asked anybody to come forward and tell of their experience of that healing. She wanted God to get all the glory.

Fr. Tardif, Sr. Briege McKenna, and many other speakers we brought to Winnipeg always filled whatever facility we rented. Fr. Robert DeGrandis, Fr. Tom Forrest were also among them. We rented the Centennial Concert Hall several times with large crowds attending.

I remember a speaker we had from Malta named Henry Cappello. He and his team traveled all over the world evangelizing. Once, they went to Borneo, which was unsafe for Christians at the time. They ventured into the jungle but struggled to make progress because the tribal leaders were not favorable to them.

In one group they visited, the chief's wife was sick. Henry and his team prayed over her, and she was instantly healed. This miracle opened doors for them, allowing them to minister throughout that part of the country. The tribes became receptive to their message and were evangelized.

That experience was somewhat like one involving Fr. Emiliano Tardif. Fr. Tardif was working in a parish in the Dominican Republic when he became very ill. He was sent to a hospital in Montreal, Quebec for treatment, and the doctors told him he might have to stay in the hospital for a year and might never be healthy again.

A group of five charismatics heard about him and came to the hospital to pray for him. Fr. Tardif, an intellectual man and a skeptic of the charismatics, believed that the solutions to all the world's problems lay in social justice. When the group asked if they could pray for him, he hesitantly agreed but asked them to close the door as he didn't want anyone to see. The Holy Spirit had other plans, and he was instantly healed.

His superior mentioned that a priest in the Dominican Republic was taking a few months off and asked Fr. Tardif if he would replace him. Fr. Tardif asked if he could start a prayer group there. The priest, skeptical of the Charismatic Renewal, reluctantly agreed. At the first prayer meeting, 200 people showed up. The people had such faith that they brought a cripple on a stretcher. His leg was broken, and he hadn't walked for 5 ½ years. He was instantly healed, along with 12 others that night.

The next week, 3,000 people showed up. A well-known lady who had been blind for 10 years was instantly healed, along with others. The following week, 7,000 people came. The police officers asked their chief to stop these gatherings because they were causing traffic problems. However, the police chief's wife, who had been sick for 12 years, was healed the previous week.

People who had not been attending Mass started

coming back, and a Catholic revival was happening. The next week, 20,000 people showed up. The Lord healed a paralyzed policeman and the deaf were healed. After five weeks, 42,000 people came to the prayer meeting which was held outside.

When the pastor of this parish returned from his time off, it was a completely different parish. Fr. Tardif began traveling around the world, visiting Winnipeg twice. He made 20 world tours in the healing and evangelization ministry, filling stadiums. He is now being considered for beatification. That's what the power of Pentecost can do.

We can all be a gift to others. Surrender your gifts to the Lord and watch Him do great things through you.

Witnessing Wonders: A Faith-Filled Week in New Orleans

We attended a conference in New Orleans, Louisiana where the hospitality was incredible. The locals were so kind that they gave us their home to stay in for a week while they moved into someone else's home. The event was spread across various hotels, with shuttle buses taking attendees to different presentations. We had many choices of sessions to attend.

In the evenings, we all gathered at the Superdome. It was absolutely amazing to be there with 50,000 people praising the Lord—it sent chills up our spines. One of the speakers was Reinhard Bonnke, who ministered extensively in Africa, drawing hundreds of thousands of people to his rallies. I remember him saying during one of his presentations that Jesus is alive today and His word is alive today; it's not just 2,000 years old but relevant right now. We witnessed people getting out of wheelchairs and the blind seeing. It was the most exciting conference I have ever attended. We came home with our faith supercharged.

Another speaker was Ernestine Reems, the pastor of a church in Oakland, California. She noticed that many people weren't coming to church, so she decided to take the church to them by going to bars and pubs. In one instance, they spoke to a lady who was in the bar to kill her husband. Instead, she had a conversion experience. The Lord is so good.

After witnessing all that the Lord was doing for His people, it was almost impossible not to be an optimist in your faith. Natalie is a wonderful optimist, like someone who falls into a puddle of muddy water and checks their pockets to see if there are any fish there.

Flying Through Fear: Trusting God in Turbulent Times

I had many fears in my life, and the Lord gave me numerous opportunities to overcome them. One reason for these fears might have been my experiences as a child walking alone through the bush with wild horses, cows, and bulls.

One of our sons, David, lived in Seattle, and there was an aggressive dog in the yard across the street. The dog would charge at us full blast whenever we walked by, only to skid to a stop, raising a cloud of dust. That made our heart skip a beat. We didn't know at the time that there was an electric fence in the ground that would shock him if he crossed it. This fence trained him to stop just before the line.

My first time flying, I was really scared. Once I was in the air, I discovered it wasn't so bad after all. Another time, the pilot came on the speaker system and said, "I have bad news." That could have been announced differently and saved some anxiety because the bad news was that we had to circle Denver for awhile.

Once, our plane took a steep dive after taking off from the Minneapolis Airport. The pilot later explained over the intercom that there had been a plane above us, and he apologized for the maneuver to avoid it.

On another flight to California, a relative called a couple of days before our trip and warned us not to fly because they had a dream, and the last time they had such a dream, the person died. That warning really got our attention, but we decided to fly anyway, trusting that the Lord would look after us. During one leg of the flight, we pulled out of the loading spot and then returned. The pilot announced that there was a problem with the plane, and they needed to fix it.

Another time, we were flying through a total whiteout and were told we would dip down to try to land, but if we couldn't, we'd take off again and go to another city.

When we face valleys in our lives, walking through them strengthens us. Flying now is much more comfortable. I can read, sleep, eat and walk around while flying.

Today is the tomorrow that you spend your time worrying about yesterday.

Going With the Flow: Unexpected Challenges in Ministry

I remember one time we invited a priest, Fr. Robert Faricy, for a weekend event. Fr. was arriving on a Friday evening at 5:30 and we were to start the seminar at 7:30. The traveling time to the location was about 30 minutes. So, we had everything all planned out that we would pick Fr. Robert up at the airport, I would bring him home and Natalie would have supper ready. We would eat and then quickly go to the conference site.

When Fr. Robert arrived at the airport, he said, "Richard you've got to take me to a doctor." My first thought was we are in such a tight schedule, my second thought was he's from the USA and he doesn't have any medical in Canada. I asked him why he needed to see a doctor. He said, "Well, my baggage got lost and my pills that I need to take were in that suitcase." I asked him what pills he needed. He said, "At least I need a baby aspirin." I said, "No problem, I've got baby aspirins." He said, "I also need a clerical shirt." I said, "No problem, my brother's a priest. I'll get you a clerical shirt." "Well," he said, "I need undershorts and socks too." I said, "No problem, I will give you that." He said, "I need a toothbrush and toothpaste." I said, "No problem, I've got a brand-new toothbrush and toothpaste. I'll give it to you."

We got him home, had supper, headed to the conference site and we were on time. During the conference Fr. told all the people there that he was wearing my undershorts and my socks. We all had a good laugh about that.

During these years we had to learn to go with the flow.

One year we had booked a priest, Fr. Jim Nisbet, from California to give us a Bible study on the Book of Revelation. He was supposed to arrive on a Sunday evening, so I went to the airport to pick him up. He was not on the plane. I phoned his home in California, and they said he's gone. He lived on the coast, and he had to drive 200 miles to Los Angeles to catch his flight. I had all these thoughts that he probably drove off a cliff in an accident, etc., etc. The next morning, Fr. Jim called me and says, "I understand you called me yesterday." I said, "Yes, I went to the airport to pick you up and you weren't there." He asked, "Was I supposed to come yesterday?" When I said, "Yes." He quickly said, "I'll get back to you. I'm on my way."

So, we didn't know what was happening. That first night we showed a video on the Summary of the Book of Revelation by another priest. Fr. Jim arrived the next day. He went to the airport in Los Angeles with a day-old ticket and they let him on the plane. In Calgary, same thing; he got on with an expired ticket. God works all things to the good.

Once, we had booked Fr. John Hampsch from Los Angeles to lead a weekend retreat. When we went to the airport to pick him up, he wasn't there. We called him, and he explained that he had missed his flight by five minutes. That evening, we had 700 people waiting in the church to hear him speak. Fortunately, we had a video on the topic he was going to teach, so we showed that to the attendees. For the rest of the weekend, they were able to hear his talks in person.

From Tabernacle to the Table: Inspiring Stories of Faith

We attended a conference in Minneapolis where we heard a powerful testimony by Fr. Mark Stang from Minnesota. We invited him to Winnipeg for a breakfast testimony, a healing Mass, and some talks. When he arrived, he asked if I could take him to the church so he could sit before the Tabernacle. I took him to our parish, and he said he would call me when he was ready to return.

He had a pad and pencil with him, and I jokingly asked if he was waiting for Jesus to give him a message. He replied, "Yes, actually I am." Five hours later, he called and said he was ready to come back. That evening, the service was unbelievable. The presence of the Lord was so powerful that you couldn't miss it.

At that same conference in Minneapolis, we heard Sr. Jean Thuerauf give her testimony. It was wonderful to see how the Lord worked in her life. Sr. Jean was working in a poor section of Minneapolis. One Monday, she told the Lord that it was O.K. for her to be alone on Good Friday but not on Easter. She felt God telling her to invite a family with 16 children for Easter dinner. This family had faced many hardships over the winter and needed some hope.

Her first thought was, "How can I invite them? I

don't have enough food, and how can I fit them all into my dining room?" She heard the words, "Trust me." She wrote a letter of invitation, as the family had no phone, and asked the Lord to send someone to deliver it. Just as she sealed the envelope, two boys appeared at the door asking if they could do anything for her. They took the letter, and shortly after, two ladies arrived with groceries. When Sr. Jean saw potatoes in one bag, she knew the Lord was providing.

Later, she realized she had no meat for dinner, but it was only two o'clock, so there was still time. Minutes later, a lady called to say her husband would be bringing an Easter gift—a small ham! Now everything was set except for dessert. As Sr. Jean was heading out the door to attend the Easter Vigil service, the phone rang. A lady said she had baked a cake for them, and her sister was bringing some ice cream. Sr. Jean marveled at how beautifully everything had come together, even without planning a menu.

Another time, Sr. Jean was awakened by voices outside her open window, which seemed too close for comfort. She jumped out of bed but saw no one; the would-be burglars had disappeared into the darkness. She prayed, "Lord, if you would send me an air conditioner for this bedroom, I could lock the windows, get some rest, and be ready to do your work tomorrow." The next morning, Tom, a friend from Golden Valley, called and said, "Sister, I was in the garage this morning and noticed an air conditioner we are no longer using. It's a small one and would fit in your bedroom window."

Commanding the Storm: A Tale of Faith and Courage

I remember one time we were in Fargo, North Dakota heading back home from a holiday, and we stopped at a service station to fill up with gas. The radio warned that a tornado was imminent in Fargo and Grand Forks. We thought, if we stay, there's a risk of a tornado, and if we go further, there's also a risk.

Faith rose up in Natalie's heart. She remembered the passage where God stretched out his hand. She stretched out her hand and commanded the storm to stop and we continued our trip.

It was just like the parting of the Red Sea. On the

road to our left were very black clouds, rain with thunder and lightning. To our right, it actually looked like a wall made of rain. Amazingly, the road ahead was clear.

Trusting God's Call: The Walls of Jericho Come Down

Any time we received a call asking us to come out and speak or pray we would always say yes because we felt that God was using that person to invite us to do his work. We didn't want to ever say no to the Lord. One day, I answered the phone and found a nun on the other end. She said, "Richard, Father has asked me to invite you and Natalie to lead a two-day retreat at our parish. Would you come?" I checked my calendar, saw that the dates were free, and agreed. After hanging up, I turned to Natalie and said, "Natalie, we're in trouble." We had never led a parish retreat before, let alone one where we were the sole speakers responsible for developing the theme and all the talks.

We began with prayer, and as we planned and prepared, everything fell into place smoothly. Before we left, a group prayed over us and shared a prophetic word that "the walls of Jericho would come down."

We could see God working after the first day of the retreat. At the end of the evening, I told everyone, "We'll see you tomorrow. Come expecting a miracle." Immediately, I thought, "What have I done? Why did I say that? Now we're really in trouble." But the words had just slipped out.

By the end of the retreat, people were crying and hugging each other. The nun said that "the walls of Jericho had come down," and it was miraculous to witness the transformation in relationships. We felt incredibly blessed and excited to see what the Lord had done, despite our initial feelings of inadequacy.

God will never call us without equipping us. I challenge everyone to discover their gifts, explore their possibilities, and be open to serving the Lord in any way He calls. When we're involved in the Lord's work, we need to take risks and encourage one another. It's truly a privilege and an honor to serve the Lord in any capacity.

From Strings to Praise: My Journey as a Worship Leader

I always wanted to learn to play the guitar. Often, we struggled to find worship leaders for the seminars we spoke at. One day, a flyer from a nearby music studio appeared in our mailbox, offering the use of a guitar and eight sessions for $89.00. I decided to enroll.

Each week, I received a lesson that seemed too difficult at first, but after practicing all week, I was able to pass the test and move on to the next one. I completed these sessions and advanced to a more challenging course.

One day, a prayer group asked me to lead their praise and worship session. This was the first time that I played for a group. They got ahead of me in the singing, and I struggled to catch up. It felt like the session lasted three weeks. At the end of the evening, several people complimented me on how good the praise and worship was. That night, I went home with a terrible headache. However, the encouragement I received inspired me to continue. I went on to lead worship for twenty-five years, never having to worry about finding someone to lead worship at our many seminars.

I knew that the Lord was the inspiration for me, and this was in His plan.

Faithful Influences: Stories of Love and Devotion

My outlook on life and priorities changed dramatically when our son Wayne passed away. Tragedy has a way of making you reflect on what truly matters. When our lives end, what will remain besides a box of pictures? Perhaps the Holy Spirit is calling you today to invite Him into your heart. It can be as simple as saying, "Holy Spirit, I need You. I surrender my life to You. Please come into my heart." I found the happiest time in my life when I surrendered to the Holy Spirit.

There's a story about a man who arrived at the gates of heaven and asked St. Peter if he could enter. St. Peter replied, "I'm looking in the Book of Life, and I don't see anything significant that you've done." The man said, "Well, I once encountered a motorcycle gang on the highway who were beating up an elderly lady. I stopped my car, got out, and really gave it to those guys." St. Peter asked, "When did this happen?" The man replied, "About two minutes ago."

I thank God for the many good people he put on our path.

Being married with children and attending a Catholic parish, a couple of priests stood out as great examples to me. One was Fr. Driscoll. He was a wonderful example to our children and us. During difficult financial struggles when one of our houses wouldn't sell, he came over and said he would offer ten Masses for us to be free of this burden. When our son was in the hospital, he came there and sat with us, providing comfort during that tragic time and visiting us after Wayne died.

Reflecting on our family life, my brother, Msgr. Stan, has always been a significant influence on me. He's kind, generous, and easygoing. He always gave us wonderful Christmas presents. As a schoolteacher, he exemplified someone who, through both good and difficult times, kept his focus on the Lord and never harbored negative feelings towards anyone.

I also think of my grandparents, devoted Catholics who lived their faith. My grandfather attended Mass every day, arriving early to sweep the steps and clear the snow at St. Ignatius Church. My parents, despite life's struggles, always held onto their faith, especially my mother. They were always willing to help me in any way they could. I remember my father, over 80 years old, helping me put in a lawn in 80-degree weather.

Throughout the years, I've met many faithful people in prayer groups. One gentleman, Lorne, never spoke a negative word about anyone in all the years I knew him. He was always positive. Before joining the prayer groups, he would break his golf clubs if he made a bad shot and said that when he spat on the ground, the grass would die. But once touched by the Lord, he became a completely new person. Many people I've met have shown their faith through their actions.

Of course, a wonderful example of faith is my wife, Natalie. She is always positive and has never harbored negative words for anyone, including me. She has a real fire in her soul for God and has been a witness to me throughout our many years of marriage. Her daily prayer life is also a testament to her faith. She lives a life of both Mary and Martha, always doing things for me. My closet is always full of clean clothes, and if I ask for a favorite meal or dessert, it's soon on the table. How could this not help me live my faith?

I once stayed at a prayer group leader's home in Calgary and could sense the Lord's presence there. Every morning, I would hear the man of the house reading Psalms of praise aloud for about half an hour. His example of a lifestyle of praise and worship really spoke to me.

I recall visiting a group hosting a leaders' seminar in New Jersey where I met a school principal who was overjoyed to serve the Lord that weekend by picking up garbage and keeping the floors clean. He was so cheerful and thankful for the opportunity to serve in any way, just to be part of what God was doing. Visible signs of joyful service like this reinforced my commitment to serve God in the same way.

I remember when our son died, a fellow from the community came over, gave me a big hug and told me he loved me, and he cried with me. I will never forget that moment. Sometimes when someone is going through grief, we just don't know what to say to them. This man knew exactly what to say and ministered to me in a wonderful way.

Eugene Wiesner was a speaker from Billings, Montana. He made a statement that still stays with me many years later. He said, "Will you still follow the Lord if he takes the cookies away?"

A Vision of the Father: Finding Love in Pesos

I would like to share a story about how God showed me and convinced me of His love. Natalie and I attended a month-long spiritual direction course at a monastery in Pecos, New Mexico. While there, I had a dream. Dreams are biblical and often bring up things from our subconscious that we may not even know exist. Most of our dreams, even if they involve others, are about ourselves.

While we were away in Pecos, I had a house under construction for a client. I asked someone to take charge while we were away. In my dream, I returned to

Winnipeg and went to the house being built. The front of the house looked older, not newly built, and instead of a nice earth-tone front with brick, it was completely painted barn red. Inside, vinyl had been laid over the floor before it was cleaned of wood chips, causing bumps to show through. Three bricklayers were working at the back of the house, putting up bricks there instead of at the front. The bricks were a mixture of colors, and the bricklayers had separated all the colors and put them in rows. The bay window in the front of the house was lopsided. There was a pedestal sink, but the top was gone. The porch was about three inches lower than the main floor, and the floor was tiled over and cracked due to the drop. The front door was elegant, with beautiful wood and beveled glass lined with gold. The fireplace was placed in the center of the room instead of against the wall. A tall, skinny fellow was spray-painting everything red—the walls, the furniture, everything. Red is often seen as the color of love.

I went over to him, put my arm on his shoulder, and said, "This is terrible. Why did you ever do this to the house? What is the owner going to say?" He replied,

"The owner wanted it just this way.   He picked everything out like this."

We all had a spiritual director, and mine interpreted this dream for me. She said that when you dream about a house, it's about yourself. I saw all these different things in the house that were wrong and done incorrectly, reflecting how I felt about myself.   The owner of the house is the Lord, and He said, "That's exactly how I wanted you, just as you are. I love you. I am pleased with you." This dream was a revelation to me and brought me to tears when I understood what God was trying to tell me.

After attending this retreat for a few days, I had a vision of God the Father during Mass. He appeared as a kind, roly-poly figure with a beautiful, gentle face, a white beard, and wearing gold and red robes.   His appearance was loving and gentle, with a heart of gold. A few days later, a priest arrived who reminded me of this vision. He was also roly-poly and had a beautiful, loving demeanor. His name was Fr. Bert.

Shortly after, the community put on a concert, but I didn't attend because I wasn't feeling well.   Instead, I went to the chapel to pray and talk to God the Father. Before leaving the chapel, I said to God, "I know you love me, but it would be nice if you could send me another sign of your love." I then went up to my room and lay down. Ten or fifteen minutes later, there was a knock at the door. It was Fr. Bert. He said he had felt an urge to come and pray for me and just had to come. I told him that I had prayed for a sign of God's love just fifteen minutes earlier. We both had tears in our eyes. God was speaking to me through Fr. Bert, reaffirming His love for me.

Proud Parents: Celebrating the Faith and Achievements of Our Sons

We are incredibly proud of our sons.

Our oldest son, David, is a man of faith. When he was an executive for Microsoft in Seattle, he kept a Bible open on his desk and wore a lapel pin that sparked conversations about Jesus. He played guitar with church groups in Winnipeg and Seattle and has witnessed to many people. Now, he helps us livestream a prayer meeting online every Wednesday evening.

Recently, he was invited to speak at Liberty University, where he mentored roughly 200 students over three days. There were 700 CEOs at the CEO Summit. David spoke at the event and shared what it means to live out your faith in the workplace.

Fr. Rick, our second son, is a priest with the Companions of the Cross. He studied Sacred Scripture in Rome and Jerusalem. When he graduated from the Hebrew University of Jerusalem and the Pontifical Biblical Institute on January 26, 1995, we were so blessed to be there. The students were from all over the world, and it was touching to hear all the priests sing. We were the only parents who had attended in the program's 20-year history. Today, Fr. Rick serves as Treasurer General, Member of the Executive Council, Member of the Formation Team, and local Superior at Visitation House in Detroit, Michigan.

Our youngest son, Gerry, is a doctor in Roseburg, Oregon. His practice is full, and his patients always tell us how much they like him and that we have a good son. While training in rural Manitoba, Gerry laid hands and prayed for a newborn child for whom things did not look good and within two days, the child made a miraculous recovery. In Vancouver, he witnessed to a dying patient who had not attended church for years, encouraging him to see a priest and make peace with God.

We are truly blessed by our sons, their wives, our grandchildren and our great-grandchildren.

Our four bundles of joy

NATALIE

Walking in His Footsteps: A Divine Tour at St. Peter's Primary Church

God will even provide you with a tour guide. When we were by the Sea of Galilee, where Jesus appeared to the disciples after His resurrection, we saw a tour guide reading a Scripture passage to a group. I thought, wouldn't it be great to have a tour guide to explain what we're seeing? Just then, a Franciscan priest who was raking up some debris came over, started talking to us, and asked if we would like him to show us around. Oh, wouldn't we!

There was a tiny, vacant church called the Church of St. Peter's Primacy. The church had a side door leading to a flat rock at the water's edge. Inside, there was a picture of a Pope on this rock. I was overwhelmed when the Franciscan priest unlocked the door and invited us to step onto this blessed rock. This is where Jesus would have stood and invited the disciples, who were fishing, for a morning fish fry. The Lord knows your every thought. How blessed we were!

God's tour guide showed us where people would

have sat on the hill to hear Jesus speak, pointing out the spot's excellent acoustics. He also showed us a cave on the side of the hill, saying, "That's probably where Jesus spent the nights in prayer because it's the only cave around here."

From Garbage to Grace: Stories of Hope in Juarez

I will never forget our trip to Juarez, Mexico, in 1987. We visited the garbage dump where people lived, and where God had multiplied food and where there were many conversions. A prayer group decided to provide a Christmas lunch for the poor living and working in the dump on Christmas Day 1972. They prepared food for 125 people, but 350 showed up. The ham was sliced and sliced and grew no smaller. The pile of fruit did not seem to go down. All 350 people had enough to eat, and they even took some leftover food home. Since then that miracle of food multiplication has happened many times.

Martha Medrano took us and our friends, Lori Ann and Rene, to the dump. We first stopped at a compound on the outskirts, built for distributing donated food and clothing to the poor. We were amazed to see the people's faces all lit up with joy. They were all smiling as we approached them, and all came and hugged us.

One of the ladies pointed to an open bag of beans and said, "You see that bag? All morning people have been helping themselves to the beans, and the amount hasn't gone down."

Manuel, a man about 30 years old, invited us to see his house. He had been a feared gang leader before his dramatic conversion to the Lord. We walked past many makeshift houses, most made of boards slapped together. Manuel's home was about 6 feet by 10 feet, made of old boards with a piece of poly vapour barrier thrown on top for a roof with pieces of scrap iron to hold it down in the wind. It was attached to someone else's house like a lean-to. The floor was sandy ground, and the door was a cloth covering the opening. An old mattress on the sand served as a bed for Manuel, his pregnant wife, and their child. There was a shortage of water, and they could only get a limited amount each day from the compound. Despite this, their clothes were sparkling white.

Manuel couldn't find work, but he learned to make adobe bricks. He hoped to build houses for others and showed us a few bricks laid out on the ground. Someday, this would be their new home.

Richard asked Manuel if he was happy. He pointed to the sky and said, "Happy. Jesus."

RICHARD

God's Everlasting Love: A Miracle at the Wailing Wall

When Fr. Stephen Barham was in Winnipeg, he told us about a man experiencing God's love through answered prayer. He said the Jews believed that the glory of God, the Shekinah, was in the temple where the Ark was. When the temple was destroyed by Titus in 70 AD, the question arose: where did the glory go? The Jews believed that the glory of God must be at the foundations of the outer wall. They uncovered those foundations, which is now the famous Wailing Wall in Jerusalem. It has become like a synagogue where people go to place written petitions into the cracks between the rocks, leaving them there for God.

One day, a guide was taking some tourists by the Wailing Wall and saw a man collapse at the wall. The guide watched as paramedics came and took him away. At the end of the day, after the tour was finished, the guide went to a sidewalk café by the Jaffa Gate. There, he saw the man who had collapsed by the Wailing Wall. The guide approached him and asked, "Aren't you the man who collapsed at the Wailing Wall today?" The man replied, "Yes, my friend. You must hear what happened. Years ago, I was separated from my son. I have searched all over the world but never found him. I came here as a good Jew to ask God for my son. When I pushed my message into the rock, another message fell out. I know we're not supposed to read them, but a voice thundered in me, 'Read it.' So, I opened it. It was from my son, looking for me, and it had his phone number. Overcome, I collapsed. But I called my son, and he is flying to Tel Aviv from Europe tomorrow. We will be together again because the God of Israel is alive and heard my prayer. His love is truly everlasting to the thousandth generation."

NATALIE

Heavenly Signs: Eucharistic Miracles and the Missionary

Image

Life-sized images of Our Lady of Guadalupe have traveled to all the states in the U.S. Richard was invited to Warroad, Minnesota, to give a talk and see the Missionary Image. I read that many people felt heartbeats when they touched the image. The original Tilma of Our Lady of Guadalupe shows she was pregnant. When I read that, I really wanted to feel the kick of Jesus. I was a bit hesitant and fearful, but I decided to try. I very hesitantly placed my hand on the image of our Blessed Mother. And boom, one big kick.

I looked around to see if there was a draft or something that caused it, but there was none. It was real. That evening, many saw the image shed tears.

Over the centuries, there have been many miracles of the Eucharist. When we were in Italy in 1995, Fr. Faricy suggested we visit a more recent one. He recommended we go to Moscufo to see Fr. Fulvio di Fulvio, who experienced this miracle while celebrating Mass twice in Verona and twice in Pescara in 1976 and 1977.

We didn't hesitate. We rented a car and drove across Italy from Rome to Moscufo. There, we saw a large host with the figure of Jesus on the cross imprinted on it. When it was consecrated, blood flowed from all the wounds of Jesus on the imprint.

We asked Fr. di Fulvio why he thought this miracle occurred. He said, "It's a sign of Jesus' faithfulness, mercy, and life. His blood washes us clean. We go to confession, and yet, we come out with no joy on our faces. We continue to carry our guilt. We should be a happy people because of what His blood does for us. God wants to remind us of this, and we are to believe it and proclaim it."

Blessed Beyond the Bumps

God has been so good to us. Sure, we have had many bumps on the road, yet He has been with us through them all. God is alive!

Printed in the USA
CPSIA information can be obtained
at www.ICGtesting.com
JSHW010801231124
74182JS00003B/12